RUN
TOWARD
THE
NIGHTLAND

Magic of the Oklahoma Cherokees

JACK FREDERICK KILPATRICK
ANNA GRITTS KILPATRICK

Southern Methodist University Press : Dallas

© 1967 : SOUTHERN METHODIST UNIVERSITY PRESS
DALLAS, TEXAS

Library of Congress Catalog Card Number 67-19814

Jack Frederick Kilpatrick, 1915-1967: A Memorial Preface

ON FEBRUARY 22, 1967, Jack Frederick Kilpatrick suffered a fatal heart attack at Muskogee, Oklahoma, only a few miles from Stilwell, where he was born on September 23, 1915. He was buried, as he had requested, in the Echota Cemetery — of whose history he had written more than once — in a little valley among the hills of the Cherokee country that he, himself a Cherokee, deeply loved.

Jack Kilpatrick was a man of many talents and of several careers, pursued simultaneously and with the passion of a nature that combined ardor with scholarliness. His formal education was in music: he held the Bachelor of Music degree from the University of Redlands, the Master of Music from the Catholic University of America, and the Doctor of Music from Redlands. Composing was one of his careers, and in this he was so successful that Leopold Stokowski called him America's greatest composer. His compositions — there are some 168, among them symphonies, an opera, and the music for six historical dramas — all contain and convey the feeling of

v

which he wrote in a letter to a friend: "I think the burden of my song has been this immemorial land, lying long in the sun — not Indians, not the United States — something that was, and is, and always will be set apart, unique, the incredible and precious creation of geology, the only home of Ancient Spirits."

His second career was that of teacher. He joined the music faculty of Southern Methodist University in 1946 and taught there the rest of his life, becoming a full professor and chairman of the Department of Music in the College of Arts and Sciences. In 1963 S.M.U.'s chapter of Phi Beta Kappa elected him to honorary membership, and in 1964 the university's Alumni Association presented him with its Distinguished Faculty Award. These official honors expressed the love and respect in which he was held by his colleagues and his students. To his friends on the campus he was a perpetual source of encouragement, stimulation, and delight. The flashing humor of the storytelling of which he was a master illuminated insights in a manner so warm, so richly human, and at the same time so unpretentious that only afterward, sometimes, did one realize what a breadth of knowledge and depth of wisdom had been revealed.

Though he gave friendship of a rare quality to people of all colors, closest to his heart always were his own people, the Cherokees. His love for them led him into his third career, that of writer. As the years went by and fewer and fewer remained who had a real command of the ancient Cherokee tongue, he was more and more driven by the intensity of his desire to preserve and record the treasures of the Cherokee culture. Shortly before his death he wrote: "Recently I read in the *Ency-clopaedia Britannica* that no native American society north of Mexico had produced a literature; yet during the past five years alone I have collected from attics, barns, caves, and jars buried in the ground some ten thousand poetical texts, many of which would excite the envy of a Hafiz or a Li Tai Po."

With his wife, Anna, he worked with an increasing sense of urgency to translate these texts and see them issued in book form. The folktales of *Friends of Thunder* were published, the love incantations of *Walk in Your Soul,* and then came the magical texts of the present volume, which he saw in page proof only a few days before his death. In another vein, there were the prose documents gathered in *The Shadow of Sequoyah.* But his thoughts were always of what remained to be done. It was not alone that the ten thousand texts were beautiful, and that the world should see their beauty. Still greater was the need for the vision they contained, the "precious gifts to all men," as he wrote, the "peace that comes from an ancient wisdom," the realizations that might spring from awareness of "as airy and sunny and buoyant a faith as was ever conceived by man."

In 1959, Jack Frederick Kilpatrick received the second citation ever given by the Cherokee Nation, "for exceptional contribution and achievement in music and the drama and exemplary service to the cultural welfare of the Cherokee Nation." The first citation had been awarded in 1824 — to the great Sequoyah, for his syllabary that gave the Cherokees a written language. In presenting the second citation more than a century later, the Chief of the Cherokees said, "Another Sequoyah has arisen among the Cherokees."

In a small volume of moving beauty, *Sequoyah of Earth and Intellect,* Jack Kilpatrick wrote of his spiritual ancestor in these words which apply no less to himself:

But to fellow Cherokees, the scholar was but a part of the man. They saw, and still see in Sequoyah the flowering in fire of the very spirit of an ancient culture. Balance and synthesis, and the acceptance of the non-material nature of existence lie at the foundation of the Cherokee thought-world. . . . One suffers the onslaughts of man and nature with dignity, and enjoys one's triumphs with restraint. The patience of the spider must be learned, and the leap of the panther must be learned. One stands and bends. The gift of life is to be spent, not expended.

In Jack Kilpatrick that spirit flowered again in the same fire. He spent the gift of life in complete dedication and with utter generosity.

MARGARET L. HARTLEY

Southern Methodist University
March 23, 1967

Run Toward the Nightland

Acknowledgment

The authors acknowledge with gratitude that certain phases of the research necessary for the preparation of this book were made possible by the financial support of the National Science Foundation.

JACK FREDERICK KILPATRICK
ANNA GRITTS KILPATRICK

Contents

Cherokee Magic

Cherokee Magic

I

Magic in
Cherokee Life

FOR WELL over a hundred years the Oklahoma Cherokees have been writing down their magic by means of the Sequoyah syllabary in manuscript books that vary in size from tiny pocket notebooks to huge ledgers, and upon odd scraps of paper. We have seen it upon requisition forms of the Union Army, upon the back of a calendar, upon coarse wrapping paper and cardboard torn from boxes, and in the white spaces of a letter from President U. S. Grant's secretary of the interior.

Both magic and medicine are almost certain to be found commingled in a manuscript that the Cherokees

refer to by the general term *nv:wo:dhi digo:hwé:li*[1]
("medicine book [or papers]"), but also to be seen there
are such typical oddments as family demography, scrip-
tural references and extracts, drafts of letters, addresses,
grocery lists in Sequoyan and phonetic English, and a
considerable amount of mathematical doodling, for
which the Cherokees have a passion that long ago ought
to have attracted competent psychological investigation.
Side by side with an incantation to discomfit a demon
may be a set of figures that attest to the comforting fact
that the Lord's work is prospering in the Baptist Church
nearby.

Any layman may decide to preserve in writing that
magic for which he has use and which is readily available to his social class: fishing charms, a little something
to protect him in an emergency, and the like. The medicine man, whom the Cherokees call a *dida:hnvwi:sg(i)*[2]
("curer of them"), may possess a small library of manuscripts. Even the *dida:hnese:sg(i)* ("putter-in and drawer-
out of them") — a sorcerer, a "witch"[3] — may risk writing
down his criminal arcana. The literary motivation of
them all is the same: magical sayings abound in archa-
isms, ritualisms, and tricky wording, and they are hard
to remember.

If it is exceedingly difficult for one without proper
credentials to acquire a "medicine" manuscript of any
kind, even one that deals with treating the toothache,
the obstacles to be overcome in obtaining one that gives
precise instructions as to how to separate a married
couple or to befuddle a jury can well be imagined. Since
he is more than likely to be a Christian, the layman has

no desire for the rumor to reach his congregation that he is doing a little weekday witching, and he is apt to deny having any knowledge whatever of magic. The medicine man is disinclined to discuss the secrets of his profession with anyone except another medicine man, from whom he stands to learn something. And, needless to say, no *dida:hnese:sg(i)* wants to confess to being what he is.

The majority of Cherokees profess Christianity, and the attitude of that majority is essentially inimical toward the ancient tribal magic, although it is not antagonistic toward the old medicine. The dividing line between the two areas is, of course, largely determined by individual interpretation. The average Cherokee is unable to see any inconsistency in his willingness to permit the invocation of a specific bird or animal spirit for the curing of his liver and his abhorrence of having the same spirit petitioned to achieve revenge upon a personal enemy. In his opinion, a well Christian is of more worth to the Kingdom of God than a sick one, and since he is apt to hold jaundiced views on the white man's therapeutic prowess, he feels that it is his duty to avail himself of the most effective healing techniques of which he knows. But vengeance belongs to the Lord.

All magic, of course, is not considered to be of a uniformly sable hue. There is a certain air of legitimacy about magical measures taken to protect one from evil or to prevent something evil from happening. And here again we deal with individual interpretations. One person who sees no harm in using a charm to protect himself while traveling is utterly scandalized to learn that his neighbor, at present without a wife, is dabbling in love magic in order to repair the deficiency. And secure in his Christian rectitude, that neighbor is appalled to find out that a deacon, no less, in the community church did not commit the outcome of a recent lawsuit entirely to the acumen of lawyers.

Some magical practices are condemned by Christians and pagans alike. Sorcery to make a person ill, or to take his life, or to separate a man and his wife is universally abhorred and feared.

The Magical
Incantation

"Most Cherokee magical rituals consist of something that one says (or merely thinks) or sings, called the *i:gawé:sdi* ("to say, one"), and some recommended physical procedures, called the *igv́:n(e)dhi* ("to do, one"), although some have no *igv́:n(e)dhi* at all. The published literature on Cherokee magic does not recognize a fundamental truth: in any magical ritual all generative power resides in thought, and the *i:gawé:sdi*, which focuses and directs that thought, alone is inviolate. The *igv́:n(e)dhi*, which merely augments the authority of thought, or serves more effectively to apply or disseminate it, may be expanded, curtailed, altered, or dispensed with entirely in conformity with personal preference, special circumstances, or the broad general principles that govern Cherokee medico-religious practice.

"There are striking parallels between the Cherokee magical ritual and the Roman Catholic Mass. An *i:gawé:-sdi* may have its Ordinary and Proper aspects, and just as we have the *Missa solemnis* and the *Missa lecta*, so do we have Cherokee texts that may optionally be sung or spoken. And while it is true that the Cherokee shaman is no more at liberty to alter phraseology than is the celebrant of the Eucharist, certain interpolations, analogous to the tropes of the Middle Ages, are admissible.

"Most commonly these extraneous elements take the form of the repetition of a key word the sacred four times; the interjection of the supremely sacrosanct numeral seven; the insertion of the pronoun *ayv* ("I"); and a hiatus in which the reciter thinks intently upon the purpose of the ritual. These are not introduced with complete freedom, but only at certain junctures approved by custom, and they are usually indicated in manuscript texts by symbols — crosses, numerals, a series of vertical dashes, and the like.

"From the published literature one might get the impression that a particular *i:gawé:sdi* is usable for but one highly specific purpose, whereas in actuality any *i:gawé:sdi* is serviceable for any number of purposes for which its wording qualifies it."[4] What is more, a master *dida:hnvwi:sg(i)* is at perfect liberty to improvise a text if the spirit moves him to do so. A text that has descended to him through tradition he will not knowingly alter, though he may not fully understand what he is saying, but upon occasion he may elect to use only part of it.

While in terms of sheer quantity the *idi:gawé:sdi*[5] that are used for curing very greatly outnumber those of an essentially magical nature, nevertheless there exists an impressive corpus of the latter, and formerly there must have been a truly astonishing number of them. The scope

of Cherokee magic has been imperfectly perceived in the
published literature. While we present here many areas
of magical practice that have not been previously reported, to our certain knowledge this study is far from
exhaustive.

The Magical
Ritual

The chief vehicle for disseminating the power of
thought is tobacco, both the commercial variety and
Nicotiana rustica. Nowadays, the former is usually pur-
chased in stores. Twist and plug forms of it are usually
preferred, although in a circumstance where the tobacco
is to be smoked by a woman or a physically weak man,
finely cut pipe tobacco may be used because it has less
nicotine content and is more palatably adulterated than
either twist or plug. Up until a generation or so ago the
Cherokees grew a good deal of commercial tobacco of
rather high quality which, after being worked up into
twists and plugs, they smoked and chewed for pleasure,
as well as used ceremonially. They grow little of it today.

Nicotiana rustica, which they usually call *tso:lagayv́:li*[6]
("tobacco, ancient"), was never raised extensively in
Oklahoma, and in these days it is exceedingly scarce.
Since among the Western Cherokees it is used with very
great infrequency in healing,[7] and in magic most commonly for nefarious purposes, it is no easy matter to get
an upstanding *dida:hnv́wi:sg(i)* to confess that he possesses any of it, or even to admit that he knows where it
might be obtained.

Tso:lagayv́:li is not planted in a field, as is commercial tobacco; for if anyone other than its planter should see it while it is growing, its power is vitiated. It is raised in secrecy in the woods, under conditions duplicating as nearly as possible a wild state. The seeds are planted on Christmas Day or St. Valentine's Day[8] in a small patch of ground prepared by having lightning-struck wood[9] burned upon it. The occurrence of thunder on the day of its planting is considered to be an especially good omen.

Since *tso:lagayv́:li* is both very hard to come by and overwhelmingly puissant, only a minute pinch of it is generally used for any purpose. It is almost never used alone.

Tobacco has no inherent magical powers, although it possesses curative properties. It must be *go:dhlvhi:so?-hnv́:hi* ("remade, it")[10] — that is, infused with supernatural authority — before it can be used magically.

The principal factor in "remaking" tobacco is the saying (or thinking) or singing of a text over it; for this transfers the creative thought to the inert herb. The potential power of the tobacco, already magical now that it has been endowed with the generative force of the human mind, can be enhanced by strengthening measures that are not absolutely necessary for the accomplishment of the purpose for which the tobacco was "remade," but which do serve to achieve the desired end more quickly.

Dawn is held to be the juncture in day when the division between the natural and the supernatural is the most indistinct, and the projection of mundane energy into the spiritual realm most easily accomplished. Tobacco is usually "remade" at this time. In certain circumstances, rather consistently for evil purposes, the negating and de-energizing influences of dusk or midnight are desirable.

In order to take advantage of the enormous genera-tive power of running water, the bank of a stream is the most advantageous place for "working,"[11] although some conjurers prefer to perform at a spring. There are cere-monies for which rippling or bubbling water is consid-ered to be especially desirable. Divining rites, for prac-tical reasons, require the water to be still. There are some magical rituals, usually of minor nature, which are seldom enacted by water. But if a large issue is at stake, the magician sometimes does not merely "work" beside water, but also washes with it, throws it over his head, or bathes in it.

If the ceremony is performed at dawn, the celebrant almost invariably faces east, the sacred and success-giv-ing direction. In some cases, after the tobacco has been "remade" by the *i:gawé:sdi*, it is held up to the strength-ening rays of the rising sun. This is never done, at least not by a master of his craft, if the tobacco is to be used for a sinister purpose.

While certain *idi:gawé:sdi* are traditionally delivered but once, most of the texts utilized in "remaking" tobacco are reiterated for a total of four times. In some rare instances, seven times is the recommended number. Ordinarily a single morning's "working" is considered to be sufficient, yet one discovers examples in which the prescription is for four ceremonies per day, or a set of enactments for four or seven successive days. The latter types sometimes present problems to the magician if the weather must be fair in order to achieve best results, as is frequently the case. If he encounters a cloudy morning in his series, he must begin anew.

As has been correctly stated in the published literature, the saliva of an individual contains the very essence of his life-force and personality, but to a lesser degree so does his breath. Expectorating and blowing upon the tobacco, therefore, invest it with strength from the life and being of the magician. And, incidentally, the magician must be in perfect health for his magic to have any efficacy.

While an *i:gawé:sdi* is being said over it, the tobacco is customarily held in the left hand and kneaded with a counterclockwise rolling motion of the four fingers of the right hand. For any circling movement counterclockwise is the "successful" or fortunate direction. In analogy to tobacco's being "remade" at sundown or midnight and not dawn, the rolling is sometimes clockwise.

It is rather general practice for the magician to be fasting while "remaking" tobacco, but if he abstains from food all the rest of the day, the force of his magic is enormously fortified.

If the tobacco that is used contains an admixture of *tso:lagayú:li,* it is neither blown nor held up to the rays of the sun. Cedar leaves or cedar seeds are occasionally added to tobacco that is "remade" for use in repelling witches, and in addition, shredded grapevine to that prepared for the purpose of capturing the affections of a woman.

A cigarette or a cigar can be "remade" with as much success as plug, twist, or cut pipe tobacco. One has to omit the counterclockwise rolling motion used when delivering the *i:gawé:sdi*, and when the cigarette or cigar is blown, two successive puffs of air are bestowed upon the one end, two upon the other. Snuff, being too easily air-borne, is never "remade."

All "remade" tobacco is exceedingly sensitive to the malign influences emanating from a menstrual or pregnant woman, a dead person, or someone who has been in contact with a corpse, and it can be weakened or rendered impotent by its merely being in the same house with them. Actual contact is not necessary. Its power is broken if it is smoked by anyone other than the person who "remade" it or the person for whom it was prepared.

In situations of critical importance a *dida:hnawi:sg(i)* may elect to turn over the task of "remaking" tobacco to those comely and benign spirit midgets, the *yv:wi tsu:-n(a)sdí:i* ("people/small, they" — Little People).[12] The tobacco is left in the vicinity of where these beings are known to reside, usually rocky or craggy places, and the individual who placed it there is informed that the "remaking" has been accomplished by discovering that it has been moved from its original location.

"Remade" tobacco is customarily used in one of four ways: it is smoked in such proximity to the individual who is its target that the smoke actually touches that person; its smoke, sometimes on a set schedule, is merely projected toward the victim, or the direction in which he is likely to be; it is smoked in such a fashion that its fumes pervade a general area; it is not smoked, but instead placed where the person for whom it is intended comes into contact with it.

Spirits and
Color Symbolism

The spirits in Cherokee magic are invoked with logic, even though the premises upon which it is predicated are not always extant. Many of the bases for attributing certain powers to these spirits undoubtedly derive from lost myths. For example, there is a myth that apparently has been written nowhere except in the field notes of Frans M. Olbrechts that sheds light upon the authority attributed to the Kingfisher.[13] But it is obvious why protection-magic petitions the assistance of Thunder, Lightning, various fierce serpents, and the Mountain Lion, and why the lover, seeking to make himself attractive, wishes to acquire the attributes of the Redbird and those dazzling spirit birds, the *Tsugv:tsala:la* and the *Di:sdi.*[14] As might be expected, some of the spirits that are stellar in Cherokee magic appear seldom, if at all, in Cherokee medicine.

The color symbolism that we discover in both the magic and the medicine is exceedingly subtle. In a broad sense colors are affiliated with directions and stylized attributes, but the incantator applies his colors (which are seven) like a painter in order to produce a total impression, and with his palette he can make a thought-painting gradually glow, or fade into sepulchral and sinister purples, blues, and blacks. Through colors he achieves dramatic development.

Much of the vaulting nobility of the phraseology of the magical *idi:gawé:sdi* appears to transfer in translation, but the passionate life that throbs through those long and sinuous verb-forms that leap upon and joyously

wrap themselves around raw thought-material that
emerges timidly from the mind is little in evidence. The
masters of the Cherokee language who conceived the
magical *idi:gawé:sdi* created like great composers with
elements of demonic force, surpassing plasticity. What in
English are dreary little walls of word-bricks, "the Seven
Clans," "not to climb over me," and the like, in Cherokee
are sheer soarings of the human spirit, infinitely varied.

One can well understand why a magical *i:gawé:sdi*, if
not delivered in the language in which it was created, is
devoid of all power of enchantment.

Forest and Stream

Forest and Stream **II**

Success
In Hunting

THE Oklahoma Cherokees hunt very little at the present time. The protection afforded by the large state game preserves in their territory has made deer plentiful, but the Cherokees evince small interest in hunting an animal whose flesh they do not particularly esteem for food. Rabbits and quails, however, they consider worth the effort expended in procuring them, and squirrels, which provide what they consider to be the tastiest of eating, they hunt with enthusiasm.

Idi:gawé:sdi specifically applicable to hunting are exceedingly rare now, and almost nonexistent in medicine books dating back a century, although charms for good

17

luck and for divining, both of which are utilitarian in
venery, are quite plentiful. Deer hunters formerly used
a special mode of divination: Upon the night before a
hunt a piece of deer liver was placed upon the fire in the
household fireplace; the direction in which the fragment
popped out of the flames was held to be that in which
good hunting was to be had. As a fire was being kindled
in the fireplace the following morning, an *i:gawé:sdi* was
recited, and upon the hunter's return in the evening from
the chase, a small piece of deer liver or heart was offered
to the fire — to our knowledge one of the few examples
in Cherokee magic of sacrifice, a concept that is weakly
developed in Cherokee culture. Sometimes in autumn
hunts deer were lured by sumac leaves, "remade" with
a song, that were held close to the hunter's chest, partially masking his face.[1] Deer were said to be attracted
to the bright red leaves.

The magic practiced by the band of Natchez that has
lived with the Cherokees since the middle of the eight-
eenth century has long been esteemed for its potency.
Although the Natchez people in their locus at the lower
end of Tenkiller Lake have become all but indistinguish-
able from their permanent hosts, the Cherokees still conjure in the extinct Muskogean language of the Natchez,
which they undoubtedly garble unconscionably.[2]

There is a Natchez song-charm for hunting deer that
is still known and used. Not a single Cherokee has any
idea as to what he is singing, or trying to sing, other than
a conviction that somewhere in the verbal jumble there
lurk the words "a big buck." The song is sung very softly
over and over while on the lookout for deer.

M. M. ♩ = 96 circa

I- sdi- fa- tsa- si- ga i- mi- tsa

tsi- hla- hi- be- tsi- no- ma.

tsi- hla- hi- be- tsi- no- ma

tsi- hla- hi- be- tsi- no- ma

tsi- hla- hi- be- tsi- no- ma

A very simple charm from the valley of *Gi:dhahyó:hi*,[3] south of Stilwell, in Adair County, is merely said while one is out hunting for either game or estrayed livestock. It can be repeated in multiples of four recitations any number of times. The charm-user implies that his powers to seek out animals is as great as that of the bloodsucking insects named:

Horsefly! Mosquito! I am as wise as You are!

Aboriginally there must have existed a large class of *idi:gawé:sdi* for use in the manufacture of weapons of the chase and of war. A specimen of one of these is preserved in a letter from Delaware County, a charm to be said while preparing the darts used in the cane blowgun that the Cherokees call an *adhu:gwe:sdi* ("to be put to the mouth by one").

While the North Carolina Cherokees still make and use the blowgun, a weapon that is remarkably effective in hunting birds and small animals, it has all but been forgotten by their Oklahoma kinsmen. Occasionally one encounters some oldster who claims to know how to make an *adhu:gwe:sdi* and its black locust-wood darts. There is an art necessary for the task: the length of the darts in relationship to the diameter and length of the hollow must be carefully calculated, and the darts, feathered with the fuzz of cattails, must fit the tube to a nicety in order to build up the proper amount of air pressure.

The "Purple Man" addressed in this *i:gawé:sdi* is held by medicine men of today to be a spirit with essentially evil attributes, but they cannot identify him with certainty; the "*Sayi:!*" they pronounce after saying the charm four times is the onomatopoeia of a lightning flash:

Purple (*Ha!*)[4] Man from Above, You have just come to make the Brown Missiles!

You people of the Seven Clans, you are wearing the Mask of Darkness.

The Purple One has just come to do this: He has just come to strike ceaselessly in the very middle of the heart.

Without turning, he has just come to do this: He has just
come to strike ceaselessly in the very middle of the
mouth. (four times) Sayi:!

There is a notation upon this i:gawé:sdi to the effect
that for the darts to retain their powers, it is necessary
for their maker to stand them up in a corner in the house
at night.[5]

Catching Fish

The Cherokee attitude toward fish as food is rather
puzzling; for rarely does one encounter an individual
who does not have either a distinct goût for fish, or a
detestation so emphatic as to lead one to suspect that
anciently there existed certain fish taboos, possibly pecu-
liar to some clan or clans, that have not been recorded.
We know from oral sources that up until a couple of
generations or so ago fishing was done in communal
groups on the larger streams in the Cherokee Nation,
such as Baron Fork Creek in Adair County, and that
catches were dried for the winter upon pole frameworks
over hardwood fires; but we feel certain that many an
enthusiastic angler refused to eat what he caught.

The Cherokees sometimes fish by methods other than
the use of conventional hooks, casting rods, seines, and
gigs. Upon occasion they go underwater, and by means
of a large hook attached to a short handle search out and
grasp large fish that have retreated into crannies under
the banks of a stream; and, although to do so is a viola-
tion of the fish and game law, they still stupefy and take
fish by the aboriginal technique of casting sacks of

pounded buckeye root or green walnut hulls into fishing holes.

Idi:gawé:sdi to insure success in fishing are rather infrequently to be found written down. Since they are widely known to the laity, the medicine men seldom take the trouble to record them. Some of these fishing charms are to be said; others must be sung; still others require an adjunctive ritual or use of a plant.

An example of the first species, one that a fisher must say four times before putting his hook into the water, runs as follows:

> Now! Listen! You Seven Clans, come on!
>
> Now we have just brought you food.
>
> Now I throw it in.
>
> *Tsi:s! Tsi:s! Tsi:s! Tsi:s!* It was the Fishinghawk!

Fish are conceived of as being constituted into seven clans, just as are the Cherokees, but whether or not the term "clan" was once synonymous with a species, or perhaps type, of fish is something that no one now appears to know. "*Tsi:s!*" is probably an onomatopoeia for the whizzing of the fishingline through the air. The reference to the Fishinghawk is either for the purpose of deluding the fish, or else the transference of the guilt of catching and killing it to a bird spirit.

A fishing charm to be sung, recorded in an old medicine book, has these words:

> Fishinghawk, I have enough!
>
> Kingfisher, I have enough!

> Beaver, I have enough!
>
> Eagle, I have enough!

This charm was undoubtedly delivered four times. The individual who wrote it down stated that after singing the song one must make the "cry" of a catfish (*Tsu:sd(i)!*), a directive which leads one to believe that the charm was for catching this specific fish. This, too, was almost certainly to be done four times after each singing of the song. We were unable to recover the tune; it may be irretrievably lost. One wonders about the presence of the herbivorous Beaver in the company of fish-eating birds, but the Sequoyah symbols for the animal (*do:yi*) are very clearly made.

Some Cherokees employ a bit of ritual to accompany an angling *i:gawé:sdi*. An octogenarian of our acquaintance informed us that as he baits his hook with a grasshopper, crayfish, or minnow, he says:

> Now! Listen! You Seven Clans, we have just brought you this.

The first fish that he catches thereafter, no matter how large, he frees and returns to the water. Then he says:

> It was the Fishinghawk! *Tsu:sd(i)! Tsu:sd(i)! Tsu:sd(i)! Tsu:sd(i)!*

Although we have here the same "cry" of the catfish as above, this angler did not consider the efficacy of his *i:gawé:sdi* to be restricted to any one type of fish.

There is practiced a more complex piscatory ritual that necessitates the use of a double-handful or so of crayfish. The fisherman takes the crayfish in a bucket or jar to the brink of the water in which he proposes to fish. If he desires a particular kind of fish, he states the fact. He then extracts seven crayfish from the container and sets them aside, after which he recites the following *i:gawé:sdi* and blows his breath upon the crayfish that remain:

Red Fishinghawk, You have just come to make a pile of seven kinds of fish — my fish! (*seven times*)

Then Red Kingfisher, You have just come to make a pile of seven kinds of fish — my fish! (*seven times*)

This is done four times. Then the fisherman takes the crayfish that are in the container, mashes them in his hands, and tosses them into the water. The seven crayfish set aside he uses as bait.

James Mooney records a fishing *i:gawé:sdi* and ritual, in use by the North Carolina Cherokees in the 1880's,[6] that is almost identical with one incorporated into a letter in our possession. This communication, not dated but seemingly of twentieth-century origin, is from a resident of Delaware County to a relative in Cherokee County. The *i:gawé:sdi* reads:

Now! Listen! Come hear, you attenders of community meetings!

You catfish and the others will be moving about, scraping the foam with your fins.

I have come to prepare White Food for you, everywhere that you are able to move.

My saliva, not lonely, will be living blended with yours
  in the lake, where loneliness cannot go.

(My name is ⸺⸺⸺.)[7]

(Mooney's translation, by the way, is grievously inaccu-
rate.)

The Delaware County writer instructs the fishermen
to chew the root of *uhna:sde:ts(i)* *usdí:i* ("root/little"),[8]
to spit all about the spot where he intends to stand or sit
while fishing, and then to spit upon the bait. When one
uses this or a similar charm, if the aforementioned plant,
somewhat rare in Oklahoma, is not available, *no:tsi usdí:i*
("pine/little")[9] is an acceptable substitute. Its turpen-
tine-like odor strongly resembles that of "little root."

Mooney states that *yú:gwil(a)* was employed for the
above purpose in North Carolina. If an Oklahoma angler
possessed some of this precious root, he would think
deeply before expending it upon a few fish.

III

Wind and Rain

Wind and **W** Rain **III**

*Controlling
The Wind*

THE WORD-FORMS in some of the *idi:gawé:sdi* for the purpose of controlling the wind point toward this class of charms as being of greater antiquity than most of the other species still extant. This makes their translation adventurous.

Hurricanes are, of course, not unknown in that part of the Southeast where all the Cherokees formerly lived; tornadoes are common in Oklahoma where most of them now live. Usually touching down in a relatively small area, they seldom cause loss of life or extensive damage to improved property, but the thoroughness with which they destroy patches of standing timber amply evidences their ferocity.

29

If a Cherokee sees a tornado approaching, in lieu of saying anything, he may snatch off his hat and wave it up and down at the oncoming twister. This measure is considered to be a fairly effective way to cause a tornado to split up and diffuse its force; but, of course, it does not achieve results as satisfactory as does this charm which, if said, will cause the tornado to leave the reciter's vicinity:

Long Person, You have just come to say that You have just appeared.

Long Man, You have just come to say that You have just appeared.

You have just come as far as the treetops.

Both "Long Person" and "Long Man" are personifications of the wind that is diplomatically reminded of its proper sphere of operation.

We venture as an exegesis of this next example: the wind is decoyed away by being reminded that he is searching for his home village, and he is gulled into expending his force harmlessly by being told that in order to find it he will have to lift up a sizable part of a whole mountain:

You are tracking down the settlement!

You have just come to lift up the scarp of the great mountain!

Another wind-chasing *i:gawé:sdi* likens the moaning of the wind to the singing of an animal spirit, the Bear. The spirit is silenced, and, therefore, the wind is silenced:

The Bear sang: *Wo! Wo! Wo! Wo! Wo! Gi! Gi!*

He is hit in the mouth!

This final example differs from the foregoing ones in that there is a bit of ritual that accompanies it: after one says it, tobacco smoke is blown in the direction from which the wind is coming. The charm is said, and the smoke is blown four times:

Purple Bunting! (*four times*)

Purple Bluebird! (*four times*)

You are to carry Him to the mountain! (*four times*)

Corn, you are small! (*four times*)

If we are correct in considering *uwe:la*, a word which ordinarily means "his [or her] liver," to be a shortened or corrupted form of *agawe:la*, a ceremonial form of "Old Woman," the personification of corn, then the meaning of this *i:gawé:sdi* would be: "Bunting and Bluebird, in your 'purple,' or sorcerer's aspect, carry the Wind away to the mountain before he damages the young corn."[1]

Making Rain

All evidence points toward the Cherokees' having possessed *idi:gawé:sdi* for making rain while they were still living in their prehistoric seat in the normally well-watered Appalachians. Both in North Carolina, where droughts are a great rarity, and in Oklahoma, where they are frequent, the rainmaker is considered to be something of a specialist, although any first-class *dida:hnvwi:-sg(i)* is as a matter of course assumed to know how to influence the elements.

Rainmakers rank with midwives on the social scale of medico-magic. Their knowledge is evaluated as being only slightly more than that of the layman; consequently, rainmaking procedures are seldom committed to writing.

One method for divining the probability of rain is to turn loose seven crayfish in the middle of a field. If the first crustacean to move heads east, there will be rain soon; if it crawls toward the west, there will be no rain in the near future.

Another and similar procedure requires the use of a lizard. The diviner places himself some four or five feet from the brink of a small stream and then releases the reptile. If it moves toward the water, rain is in the offing; if it does not, no rain is imminent.

A simple ritual for inducing rainfall is this: An individual, man or woman, goes to a thicket beside a creek, dips out water in a turtle shell, and splashes it upon the leaves and the other vegetation nearby. There is no prescribed number of times that the water must be dipped, nor is there any specific time of day recommended for the enactment of the ritual.

A more formal rite requires the services of a rainmaker and three assistants. At sunrise all go to the west bank of a stream of considerable size. With his head toward the east, one assistant lies down toward the south. The rainmaker submerges to the bottom of the stream, lies facing east, and says:

A:tsha![2] *A:tsha!* Over there is fresh water!

Du! Du! Du! Du![3]

The submerging and the underwater recitation are done

three more times — with the head of the rainmaker successively facing north, west, and south. Upon coming to the surface after the fourth submergence, the rainmaker stands facing east and throws water over his head seven times.

The entire ritual is repeated at sundown and at midnight, and the series of three enactments is performed for four successive days.

In another rainmaking rite, before eating, the rainmaker goes to a creek at earliest dawn, takes a forked willow branch in his hand, dives into the water, shakes the branch over his head as he submerges, and while continuing to shake it over his head underwater says:

> Grandfather, I want water!
>
> Grandmother, I want water!
>
> Uncle, I want water![4]
>
> The Fish wants water!
>
> The Terrapin wants water!
>
> *Ne!*[5] Now a cloud is coming!
>
> *Ne!* Now water is coming!
>
> *So:!*[6] (*prolonged*)

This rite is enacted on four consecutive mornings.

IV

Field and Home

Field and Home

IV

Making Corn
Stand Up

THE APPARENT paucity of charms applicable to agriculture to be found among a people who traditionally have had a farming economy is somewhat puzzling. Very likely, since agricultural magic lay within the province of the laity, shamans had very little reason to record it, and having no use for it in an era of scientific farming, the laity discarded most of it decades ago.

This song-charm, found in a Cherokee County medicine man's notebook, must owe its preservation to the fact that it is "medicine" for an agricultural emergency beyond the powers of the magic of either the farmer or the county farm agent. The purpose of it is to make young corn, blown over by wind or beaten down by rain or hail, right itself.

This must be a charm of very great antiquity indeed.
While it merely approaches intelligibility, in contemporary Cherokee it would probably run something like this:

a:gwu   tsunanv́:na   wuh-
here, right   where have sat down they (alive)   over
hyé?go   u:wo:hiyúa
there it stands (hab.)   he [or she] believes

Here they [the corn-plants] have sat down.
He [or she] believes that they will be standing up.

The use of the "alive" quality instead of the generally
used "long" quality in the verb -nv- ("to sit") evidences
the attributing of a supernatural essence to corn.

The singer of the charm first faces east. Then, while
singing, he slowly walks in a counterclockwise circle that
encloses four hills of corn. He adjusts the tempo of the
song to coincide with the completion of the circle. The
ritual is enacted four times.

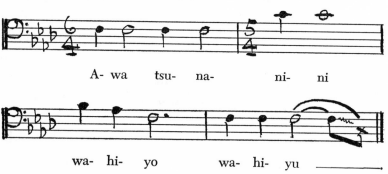

A- wa   tsu- na-   ni-   ni

wa- hi- yo   wa- hi- yu _____.

Making Food
Cook Faster

Certainly there formerly existed a large repertoire of
Cherokee household magic, but it is little in evidence in

our day. What is still viable is of a very simple character, such as is this charm to hasten the cooking of food:

I have just come to put in the Crayfish!

The clue to this seemingly enigmatic saying is the fact that a crayfish, when immersed in hot water, quickly turns red, just as does its marine relative, the lobster. This rapid change of color represents quick cooking; therefore, the *i:gawé:sdi* implies that the food on the fire has been invested with the crayfish-like attribute of getting done with dispatch.

A variant of the above runs thus:

Now! *Ha!* Now very quickly I have just come to put the Red Crayfish in the pot!

All of You speedily cook!

If household magic as such appears to have been much eroded, domestic medicine still flourishes mightily, and there exists an extensive array of conjurations appropriate to such minor accidents and ills as cuts, burns, nosebleeds, insect bites, headaches, and toothaches.

V

Traveling

Traveling **V**

Protection
While Traveling

NUMEROUS *idi:gawé:sdi* to shield one from the ancient dangers of the trail — the enemy in ambuscade, wild beasts, and the unfriendly elements — still exist. Many are superbly poetic compositions, glowing with multi-syllabic verb-forms that depict complex and minute actions with an exactitude unknown to the languages of Europe.

In the ensuing specimen, to be said four times before setting out upon the road, the speaker, addressing himself, reassures himself of the way-leading presence of the dreadful *Ugh(i)dhe:n(i)*,[1] the mythical sea-dragon of the Cherokees, and of that gigantic animal spirit, the Mountain Lion, who proudly marches before, twisting his supple neck to investigate every possibility of peril.

Now! In front of you the *Ugh(i)dhe:n(i)* will be going,
   spewing flames.

Now! In front of you the Red Mountain Lion will be
   going, his alert head reared.

(This is your name: _____.)[2]

The next example, doubtless an even more powerful
protective, replaces the great feline spirit with Lightning:

Now! On White Pathways I am making my footprints.

One will be able to see the moving feet of the
   Ugh(a)dhe:n(a)[3] going before me.

On White Pathways I am making my footprints.

The Red Lightning will be stretching out a flashing sheet
   in front of me.

Du! Du! Du! Du![4]

(My name is _____; my clan is _____.)[5]

The next specimen is illustrative of a type of protec-
tion-while-traveling charm applicable to a special circumstance — when there exists a likelihood of meeting
with personal enemies. We assume that it is to be recited
four times, although the manuscript from which it was
extracted does not so state:

From the White Mountains I originated: I am a Little
   Man.

On White Pathways I am making my footprints: the
   Blue Ones cannot do it.

Let it be raining when they will be making their footprints in the Pathway.

In the very middle of the Pathway their souls have just
   come to be cut into slices!

The statement "I am a Little Man" implies that the
traveler bestows upon himself the attributes of those wise
and resourceful immortals, the Little People. His future
is "White," *i.e.*, serene and safe, whereas that of his enemies cannot be because they are "Blue," *i.e.*, supernat-
urally fated to misfortune and defeat. In Cherokee
ritualism a soul that is "sliced" is usually tantamount to
one that is confused and indecisive.

Another special-purpose travel-*i:gawé:sdi* is this one
for being out on the road at night:

Listen! *Ha!* You have just come to hear, You Provider[6]
   who rests Above.

Ha! Now You have just come to place my feet upon the
   Brown Stone.

Ha! Let them be keeping my fine attire out of sight.

Listen! From the Sunland where You rest, You have just
   come to hear, Red Man.

Ha! Arise now!

Ha! He has just brought your soul as high as the treetops. You have just come to alight upon my right arm.

"I have just come to trace your footsteps." Listen!

The septempartite form of this beautiful *i:gawé:sdi* at-
tests to its unusual authority. Like many another charm
of comparable length, it is a miniature drama in which
all the *dramatis personae* are played by the reciter.
Stripped of its poesy, it would read something like this:

I am now going to speak: Now! You Provider from the sky, I know that You will hear what I have to say.

Yes, indeed! Now I feel that You will assure my future [the "Brown Stone" is the divining pebble, the symbol of knowledge of the future].

Just a word of caution! Do not let my enemies know that I have supernatural protection.

And I also want to say this: Thunder, You from where the sun is, I know that You will hear what I have to say.

Come on! [to himself] Keep up your spirits!

You see! [to himself] The Provider has given me encouragement. You [to the Provider] have endowed me with power.

"I [Thunder speaking] have come to protect you." This is all I have to say.

The *i:gawé:sdi* is said the usual four times.

Making a Road
Seem Short

If the Cherokees enjoy no reputation for being outstanding runners, they are extraordinary walkers. We know many an individual to whom ten or fifteen rolling and winding hill-country miles are analogous to the urbanite's stroll to the corner minute market.

There is a genre of *idi:gawé:sdi* and songs available to soften the rigors of a long walk. Some of these spirit-lifters are thought by the individuals who know them to

be applicable to any mode of traveling, even by auto-
mobile or airplane. The Sequoyah County fundamental-
ist who wrote down the following charm for us, however,
was unwilling to commit himself to the validity of any
such extension. It is to be said but once after beginning
a walk from which any turning back, once the charm is
delivered, is certain to result in an unnatural degree of
fatigue.

Now! Leech, quickly You have just come undulating
in!

Now! Leech, quickly You have just come in and balled
yourself up!

Now! Leech, quickly You have just come in and com-
pressed yourself into a mass!

Now! Hummingbird, quickly You have just come to help
me go!
Dayi:!

The transmitting into English of the consummate de-
scriptive power of Cherokee verbs is put to the supreme
test in attempting to convey the exact motions of the
"quick" Leech. *"Dayi:!"* symbolizes, of course, dazzling
speed.

A trip-shortening charm-song from Cherokee County
runs thus:

U- ne- hla- tsi-   da

yv- wi   tsi- na-   gi

nv- da- de- gwa   da- yu- le- hwa- di

a- hu- lu   a- hu- lu   a- hu- lu   a- hu- lu.

A translation of this would run:

> Provider! Provider!
> "I have just picked the person up!"
> The Big Moon is approaching in the road!
> *A:hulu! A:hulu! A:hulu! A:hulu!*

If *une:hlatsi:da* be a poetic form of *une:hlanú:hi* ("Provider"), as it would appear, then "I have just picked the person up!" would seemingly be the Voice of the Deity answering to His name and stating that He had assisted the petitioner in his walk by "picking him up." *Nv:dade:-gwa,*[7] the term for the month of November, could mean either "Big Sun" or "Big Moon" (the major heavenly bodies have the same designation in Cherokee); the indi-

vidual who knew this song, however, was of the opinion
that "Big Moon" was intended. In either case the reference remains obscure. "*A:hulu!*" is the ritualistic form of
ahu:li ("drum"). Used in the context above, it is a jog-
ging onomatopoeia.

The song is to be sung no set number of times.

Love

Love

Remaking Oneself

CHEROKEE MAGIC abounds in terms that merely skirt their true meanings. *Ado:dhlvhi:soʔdí:yi*, for example, literally means "to remake [or repair] oneself"; but a definition of the end product of the process of "remaking oneself" is hard to come by. Broadly speaking, however, as we have stated in *Walk in Your Soul* (p. 11), "a person who has 'remade' himself has surrounded the ego with a spiritual aura through which the light of the old self is brilliantly refracted." This radiance attracts the opposite sex, wealth, success, and good fortune.

There is a close relationship between the *ado:dhlvhi:-soʔdí:yi* and the *ado:du:hisoʔdí:yi* ("to rebeautify oneself") *idi:gawé:sdi*, the latter being but a subspecies of the former. The two terms are frequently interchanged.

The "to remake oneself" spells are of two classes —
those simply said, those said while "remaking tobacco,"
neither of which as a general rule necessitate any proximity to running water. Moreover, the layman can "remake" this "to remake oneself" tobacco for himself, if he
knows an *i:gawé:sdi* appropriate to the purpose.

Illustrative of the type that requires nothing but recitation is the spell below, stated four times before setting
out for the place where there is a woman that the sayer
wishes to impress:

I am dressed as well as the Redbird.
I am as handsome as the Redbird.

I am as masculine as the Redbird.
I can do as much as the Redbird.

I can say as much as the Redbird: *Dho:tsu! Dho:tsu:hwi!*

The last two words mimic the song of the redbird. *Dho:-
tsu:hwa,* the Cherokee name for this bird, appears to be
but another version of the same call.

There is an *ado:dhlvhi:so?dí:yi i:gawé:sdi* that must be
said early every morning for four days. Upon each of
those mornings the reciter faces east, wherever he hap-
pens to be, extends his arms, delivers the spell, and then
brings his arms to his body in a gathering-in gesture.
Successively facing north, west, and south, he repeats
the ritual.

This is what he says:

Gv:v! Gv:v! Red Man!

Tsugv:tsala:la,[1] I just shook the raiment from my body
   until it faded. This is my name, ————. Seven![2]

The shadow of my raiment is faded: my raiment has
faded from my body. I just shook the Raiment of the
Red Man until it faded.

Red *Dhla:nuwa*,[3] I just shook my raiment until it faded.

I just shook the raiment of the Red Man until it faded.

My body, then, is good: be thinking of me.

Then quickly, the White Chair! Quickly they have just
brought it down!

"*Gv:v!*," the onomatopoeia of the tread of the Red Man,
Thunder; the interjection of the sacrosanct numeral
seven; the White Chair of good fortune — all these are
familiar motifs in Cherokee magic. The shaking of vest-
ments is not. The explanation that most readily comes to
mind is that by shaking of the attire its magic essence
is extracted and disseminated.

Tobacco, to be smoked at any time and place that a
desired woman is present, is "remade" early in the morning (any location will do) by saying the *i:gawé:sdi* below
four times while rolling the tobacco in the usual counterclockwise manner:

I am as beautiful as the *Tsugv:tsala:la*.

I am as beautiful as the Hummingbird.

I am as beautiful as the *Dhla·nuwa*.

As the Red Cardinal is beautiful, I am beautiful.

As the Red *Dhla·nuwa* is beautiful, I am beautiful.

As the Red Redbird is beautiful, I am beautiful.

As the Blue Cardinal is beautiful, I am beautiful.

There is something peculiarly Cherokeean in the unexpected dissonance provided by the color of the Blue Cardinal among his red avian associates. That touch of blue, the hue of love-longing and loneliness, injects power into a spell said for the purpose of enduing its reciter with romantic charm.

Rebeautifying Oneself

The *ado:du:hiso?dí:yi idi:gawé:sdi* lie about halfway between those spells that would be conserved and dispensed by a *dida:hnvwi:sg(i)* and those that would be in the common knowledge of the laity. A typical example ordinarily requires but little accompanying ritual: just an expectoration upon the hands and a symbolic washing of the face (and sometimes other parts of the body also) with saliva after each of four deliveries of the words.

These spells are usually rather brief:

Now! I am a Double-man!

Ha! I alone will be the most beautiful.

This is my name, _____; this is my clan, _____.

Here is another wispy and winsome example:

Red Cardinal! *Ha!* You and I conjure!

Now Red Hummingbird! *Ha!* You and I conjure!

Now then! You and I are dressed alike!

Those beautiful spirit birds, the *Tsugv:tsala:la* and the *Di:sdi*, the latter said to be blue and very small, may be extinct avians that have been translated *galv́:la?dí* ("on high"), where they now live, on call in affairs of the heart:

Red *Tsugv꞉tsala꞉la,* I have just come to talk to every one of the women in the Seven Clan Districts.

Now! Listen! Red *Di꞉sdi,* You overpoweringly great Wizard, my soul, in the very middle, is as beautiful as the Red Lizard.

Now! All of you women in the Seven Clan Districts will be looking at me, for I alone am the most beautiful.

Somewhat similar to the foregoing is:

Now! Listen! I am as beautiful as the Red *Di꞉sdi.*
I have just come to play the male toward all of you women in the Seven Clan Districts.

Ha, then! One has come to drive away, like the Sparrow Hawk, loneliness from you Seven Peoples.

There in the very middle, as beautiful as the Red Cardinal, I have just come to speak.

Now You[4] have just come to put White Eyes into my body.[5]

If its phraseology is fundamentally appropriate, or if fitting substitutions of key words in it can be conveniently made, any "to remake oneself" or "to rebeautify oneself" *i꞉gawé꞉sdi* can be used by a female as well as a male.

Attracting a Woman

Erotic *idi꞉gawé꞉sdi* which in their day in North Carolina Mooney and Olbrechts found to be among "the

most mysterious and occult" of all incantations, are, for
some reason, exceedingly numerous in Oklahoma manuscripts. And they are frequently of striking beauty. As
is the case of a good many other classes of spells, some
need merely to be said (or sung), while others are for
the use of a *dida:hnvwi:sg(i)* in remaking tobacco for a
client. The successful conclusion of a romance being a
serious matter, it used to be that a young man would pay
a stiff price for a good love-spell; but a more modern
view appears to be ascendant now: if one invests his
money in a "to gain wealth" spell, prowess with women
somehow naturally follows!

Those spells that do not require tobacco are merely
delivered four times by the lover toward the object of
his affections, and after each statement the breath is
blown at "the middle of the breast" of the desired one.
Distance is not reckoned to be much of a factor.

Some of these *idi:gawé:sdi* are very brief, as is this one:

> Look at me very beautifully.
>
> Let us talk very beautifully.
>
> There is no loneliness —
>
> So let us talk!

Some exude confidence:

Now! Wren, I am as beautiful as You are.

You Women, I have just come to pull all of you away.

Then you all have just put White Eyes into my body: all
of you will keep your eyes on me alone.

You White Women, I have just come to pull all of you
away!

Birds figure prominently in love-incantations:

Now! I am dressed as the Redbird is dressed.
I am dressed as the Cardinal is dressed.
"Wa:gu! Wa:gu!"[6] they will say to me! *(said twice)*
"Gho:ga! Gho:ga!"[7] they will say to me! *(said twice)*

Presumably these bird calls will be twittered by enchanted young ladies.
   We have a veritable aviary in this example:

Now! Listen! *Ha!* I, who am as beautiful as the Red
   Tsugv:tsala:la, speak.
I, who am as beautiful as the Shrike, speak.
I, who am as beautiful as the Bluebird, speak.
I, who am as beautiful as the *Di:sdi,* speak.
Now! Listen! Yellow Mockingbird, I have a nest.
Then all you women, the Bluebird has just come by:
It was my body!

   And this one is of Oriental sensuousness and grace:

Now! Eagle, *Tsugv:tsala:la,* Robin, *Dhla:nuwa!*
All of You are attired in the brightest possible Red.
I am attired superior to all those in the Clan Districts.
The Eyes of your soul have just come into my body.
And now your soul has just aimed the White Red Smoke
   of the White Red Tobacco at my body.

It has just come to alight upon it.

And now my body smokes your saliva, your soul, your
   blood!

The use of "remade" tobacco in order to gain the affec-
tion of a woman in itself is considered to be a bit sinister;
but the use of *tso:lagayv́:li* to augment the power of common tobacco is regarded as both evil and perilous. Since
a woman's heart is "weaker" than that of a man, there
exists the danger that a couple of years or so later she
may fall ill from the effects of the *tso:lagayv́:li,* consult
a *dida:hnese:sg(i)*, discover who put a spell upon her,
and prevail upon the conjurer to "return the evil."

The *i:gawé:sdi* below is one used by a *dida:hnvwi:sg(i)*
to "remake" tobacco for a client who, when he smokes it,
blows the smoke toward the unresponsive woman with
whom he is in love and then imitates the calls of the dove
and the yellow mockingbird. The lover does this at dawn,
midmorning, midafternoon, and dusk.

Now! Listen! You Ancient One who rests Above, You
   fail in nothing.

Now! She comes from the _____ clan; her name is
   _____.

Now! Dove, they have just come to You from the Seven
   Clans.

You must look about You very quickly: for I am a Crow,
   and my clan is _____.

I am a man that is not lonely. Bluebird, I will keep on
   walking!

All of you women are not to think that I will be alone:

The One who lives on high has permitted me to be
attired in the Red Sunrise.

Gu:le![8] *(said four times) Huhu!*[9] *(said four times)*

"Calling like a distant bird" is the written instruction
concerning the bird calls.

The next example bears unusual directions in order to
insure extraordinary power. The tobacco itself is "remade" at sunset, not dawn, as is many times the case
when an underhanded advantage is desired. The client
goes to the bank of a stream at dawn and smokes the
tobacco toward where the desired woman lives, after
which he washes his face four times. He then smokes
again at noon and at dusk. The smoking is done for four
days.

Now! The Red Tobacco has come to strike your soul.

I have just come from the treetops: I have just come to
step over you.

Ha! Do not think it too far: face your feet this way.

Ha! Without knowing it, you have just come to my door:
let your soul be anxious.

Seven! You will be leaving your home, leading your soul
toward me.

Now tonight — Seven! — you will be thinking of me: you
will think that I am the only one living.

And I will let you go when the sun rises.

The sacred numeral seven, used as an interjection, adds
to the already overwhelming power of the tobacco; and
yet an unscrupulous *dida:hnv́wi:sg(i)*, or a *dida:hnese:-*

sg(i), might add a pinch of *tso:lagayv̇:li,* pulverized cedar berries, and shredded grapevine, thus making the tobacco transcendentally potent, and possibly fatal to the victim.

Insuring Success
With Girls at a Dance

It has been decades since the Cherokee tribal dances were performed in Oklahoma in anything approaching their traditional sequence. Most dancing today is done as an integral part of the ceremonies of the Keetoowah Society,[10] and while we know of no thorough study that has been made of it, its adulteration with elements from the choreography of the Creeks, the Natchez, and still other tribes is obvious.

The function of certain of the Cherokee dances in forwarding socially-sanctioned courtship of the young is echoed in this ritual found written in an old medicine book that probably originated somewhere in the vicinity of Blackgum Mountain, at the lower end of Tenkiller Lake. We read here that the young man desirous of being accepted by the girls attending a dance in the evening is enjoined to bathe in running water the previous dawn and to say the following *i:gawé:sdi* four times. While the directions do not so state, he would be expected to recite facing east, and upon finishing to submerge seven times.

A very interesting aspect of this *i:gawé:sdi* is the "thought" interpolations, indicated here by the sign ✕. At these junctures the celebrant pauses briefly and meditates upon what he has just said.

Listen! *Ha!* Now very quickly You have just come to hear, *Hige:hya Gu:gv.*[11]

You have just come to anoint my body with Your Red Saliva. ✗

The Blue Ones avoid me: You have just come to "re-make" for me the Red Attire. ✗

The _____ clan is attired in Blue.[12]

My footsteps have just fallen upon the Pathways.

I have just come in Full Attire.

They will be avoiding me!

Putting a Family
To Sleep

While the Cherokees are unwilling to concede that the magic of any other tribe, generally speaking, is more effective than their own, they grant that some other Indians are strong in specialties. The Creeks, for example, they regard as being especially skilful in *digá:-dhli:dhadi:sdí* ("to put them to sleep, one") conjuring. For Negro magic, oddly enough, they have no very high regard, except in the area of divining.

Creek magic to put a woman to sleep for some sinister purpose[13] is widely known, and said to be rather frequently used; Cherokee magic for the same purpose, although reputed to be exceedingly effective, is known to but few individuals, and apparently practiced but little.

There is a Cherokee *i:gawé:sdi* to "remake" tobacco for the purpose of putting to sleep not only a desired woman, but also her whole household at the same time.

There is nothing unusual in the manner in which the
tobacco is "remade" or in the fashion in which it is utilized: for the smoke of it is merely blown four times
toward the residence for which it is prepared. So potent
is the *i:gawé:sdi,* however, that it alone is used. The reciter says it four times, and after each saying of it, he
blows his breath toward the house wherein lives the
family that he wishes to become somnolent.

This is the text:

People, sleep is coming!

Very quickly all of you are turning over.

Night is coming.

Keep on throughout the night: the Dark Moon has just
    come to live in your soul!

Separating Persons

Mooney and Olbrechts take notice of the North Carolina *idi:gawé:sdi* ". . . to kindle discord and to sow ill
feeling between a married couple, or between sweet-
hearts, so that the conquest of the party desired may be
made easier by the heretofore unsuccessful lover."[14] Even
after taking into consideration the fact that Mooney and
Olbrechts are writing of the magic of the Cherokees in
North Carolina and we of that of their relatives in the
West, we suspect that these ethnographers failed to
discover that the *di:dagale:n(v)dho?dí:yi* ("to separate
them with, one") *idi:gawé:sdi,* as a class, have a wider
application than as stated above; for they are used to
create enmity between individuals who are in any state
of amity: male friends, female friends, a male and a

female in a Platonic relationship, and individuals with ties of blood, as well as lovers and spouses.

These incantations are held to be among the most evil resources of a *dida:hnese:sg(i)*, inasmuch as the wrongs they engender cannot be delimited, but can grow into bloodshed, and into family feuds that endure for generations. Every *dida:hnvwi:sg(i)*, however, no matter how reputable, has a full repertoire of these incantations. They are a part of his panoply of defense; for just as he must be prepared to deal with a single enemy who seeks to harm him or his client, so must he have the weapons to break up combinations of persons who pool their powers.

Most of the *di:dagale:n(v)dhoʔdí:yi* incantations are used in the "remaking" of tobacco in the conventional way: at daybreak, facing east upon a creek bank, with four statements of the text while kneading the tobacco with a counterclockwise rolling motion, and with the blowing of the breath upon it after each statement. It is never held up to the rays of the rising sun, however, and a sprinkling of pulverized *tso:lagayv́:li* is almost invariably used if this potent additive can be obtained. Since pre-existing enmity may permit the user of the tobacco small opportunity to blow its smoke directly upon the prospective victims, the smoke is usually blown toward where they reside, at dawn, noon, and dusk, for four consecutive days.

This "separator" is primarily for use against a man and his wife, or a pair of lovers. The names of both (the names of their clans are not necessary) are first stated: You Two Little Great Wizards, You fail in nothing.

Very quickly I have just come to tell You Two the word.

Very quickly I have just come to cut you upon your right side with the Red Knife!

Very quickly I have just come to cut you upon your left side with the Red Stick![15]

This example can be used to separate any two individuals who are first named and identified by clan:

Now! Someone has just come to frighten and separate their souls!

Somewhere upon a lonely Road in a Valley in the Wilderness your two lonely souls are to be broken!

The Cherokee word which we translate as "to frighten and separate" is one that he used to describe the action of wildlife, such as deer or quail, which flees in panic after having been suddenly come upon and startled.

Many *di:dagale:n(v)dho?dí:yi idi:gawé:sdi* are of considerably greater length than the foregoing specimens. One observes that the second part of this rather sizable bipartite incantation, one for general use involving persons of opposite sex, contains subtle deviations from the first part, differences that must be scrupulously observed in order to maintain validity:

1.

Now! Listen! *Ha!* Red Velvettail Rattlesnake, Your resting place is in the Sunland: You are a great Wizard!

Quickly I have just made it known to You.

Then quickly now You have just laid down the Pathway.

The name of the man is _____; the name of the
woman is _____. *Ha!* I have just come to place a
Post in the middle between them.

Ha! I have just come to get your saliva. *Ha!* The Red
Stick did not pursue it.

I have just come to take it away. Now it is well-guarded.

I will raise you to your feet. *Ha!* Now we are in a hurry
to go.

2.

Yellow Copperhead, Your resting place is in the South-
land: You are a great Wizard!
Ha! Quickly I have just made it known to You.
Then quickly now You have just laid down the Pathway.
The name of the man is _____; the name of the
woman is _____. *Ha!* I have just come to place a
Post in the middle between them.

Ha! I have just come to get your saliva. *Ha!* The Red
Stick did not pursue it.

I have just come to take it away. Now it is guarded.

I will raise you to your feet. *Ha!* Now we are in a hurry
to go.

Marriage

Marriage

*Acclimatizing
A Newlywed Wife*

MAGIC TO CAUSE a recently wed wife to be contented in the strange surroundings of her new home, being for a socially-accepted purpose, has no evil connotations. It is commonly called by the generic term *galá:n(i)sdoʔdí* ("to acclimatize one with, one"). Tobacco is not used with these charms; they are simply said or sung. The same *idi:gawé:sdi* that are directed toward a bride are used to allay the misgivings of newly acquired farm animals who are bewildered by their new home.

This typifies the *galá:n(i)sdoʔdí* charms:

This is what I was named, _____; this is my clan, _____.

I am a Wizard (this You[1] apportioned to me): I pass
through the souls of the people.

I am a Wizard (this You apportioned to me): I pass
through the souls of the Seven Peoples.

I am a Wizard (this You apportioned to me): I pass
through the very Sun.

I am a Wizard (this You apportioned to me): I pass
through the Moon.

I am a Wizard (this You apportioned to me).

This is what you were named, _____; this is your
clan, _____: you pretend to be a newborn baby,
and you pretend to be an old woman, but I have
already passed through your soul!

All *galá:n(i)sdoʔdí idi:gawé:sdi* are said four times, of
course. Some are quite brief, such as this one, dated
November 12, 1899:

(Your clan is_____; your name is _____.)

I just consumed your heart!

I just consumed your soul!

I just consumed your flesh!

I just consumed your saliva!

Some *gala:n(i)sdoʔdi* charms are said or sung this way:
the husband approaches the dining table after it has been
set for a meal, says his wife's name, and then delivers
the *i:gawé:sdi*.

One of the loveliest examples of a *gala:n(i)sdoʔdi* that
we can recall having seen is this one, found in a collec-

tion of loose sheets of paper near the southern border of Adair County in the highest and wildest part of Cherokeeia:

Now! Listen! *Tsugv:tsala:la*, You rest Above: You fail in nothing.

Then quickly let us take away her soul!

This is her name, _____.

Then one half of it has just become enlarged.

We have just come to blow our breaths beside the Resting Place of the Ancient White One.[2]

We have just come to bear her away from beside the Resting Places of the White Chairs.

She will live, then, in my home forever!

Compelling a Runaway
Spouse to Return

One of the functions of the *dida:hnvwi:sg(i)* is to be of service to the husband whose wife has left his bed and board and to the wife whose husband was negligent in supplying a forwarding address. This assistance can take one of several forms: divining the whereabouts of the missing mate; souring any new attachment that he or she may have formed; or conjuring up an irresistible desire in the heart of the fugitive to return to conjugal duty.

The *i:gawé:sdi* that he may choose to use in "remaking" tobacco to be used by the client in inducing an absconding mate to come home is invariably worded, as written down in medicine books, from the standpoint of the husband; but this is merely a convention: some of the spells can be used as they stand, and in others suitable substitutions of words can be made, when the client is a wife. The tobacco itself is prepared by the *dida:-hnvwi:sg(i)* in a more or less standard way: at sunup, while fasting and while standing facing east at the water's edge, and by rolling it counterclockwise while the incantation is said four times. The client takes it home and smokes it at dawn and at dusk for four days. The smoke is blown toward wherever the faithless spouse is likely to be, mentally aimed at the center of the fugitive's breast.

The fidelity of the dog is the tonic chord in this incantation: the runaway, come to her senses, will return and be as constant as a dog:

What the Black Dog does, you have just come to do.

Ha! You have just come, "remade."

You have just come, "remade."

This is your name: _____.

What the Little Dog does, You have just come to do.

You have just come, "remade."

What this White Dog does, you have just come to do.

And in another *i:gawé:sdi* we have a vivid presentation of the attractions of the abandoned mate:

I am as beautiful, then, as the Bluebird! (*four times*)

I am as beautiful as the Hummingbird! (*four times*)

The Passenger Pigeon eyes my raiment! (*four times*)

I am as beautiful as the Swan! (*four times*)

Another example makes such telling points as the self-sufficiency and masculinity of the deserted husband, and the discontent in the soul of the runaway woman who is offered a "Crow" in the person of another man, whereas she might have a "Sparrow Hawk" if she would but return home. The "He corners me! *Mi:?!*" is a tiny interpolated drama in which we hear the cry of the despicable "Crow," pursued and caught by the masterful "Sparrow Hawk," who celebrates his victory with a triumphal hawk-scream.

I came from up there Above.
Now I have just come down from where You rest, You
    Ancient White One.

I have just come around a bend in the Pathway over
    there: I am not a lonely Crow.
I have just come around the bend: it is good on this side.
Let my soul be let down from Above: let you be the one
    who greets it.

Ha! You White Woman, you hunt your lonely soul,
    which will be moving about here and there.

Ha! In a friendly fashion the Sparrow Hawk has just
    flown in.

Ha! They will be offering you the body of a Crow.
    "*Gha:?!*"
He corners me! "*Mi:?!*"

They have just come to tell me that your soul is very
    lonely.
Now and then lonely Eyes will be living with you.

I am a man! I hunt your very lonely soul that lives about
   here and there.
I am a good one! My soul will not be appearing about,
   lonely.
My body is not lonely: you will find rest in my body.

VIII

Wealth and Good Luck

Wealth and Good Luck    **VIII**

Obtaining Wealth

SHOULD ONE be impolitic enough to query the possessor of a wealth-getting *i:gawé:sdi* as to its efficacy, his answer would probably be a stare of utter astonishment; for the failure to note that the cabin of the possessor of the charm had three rooms instead of two, and that the yard was swarming with chickens of uncertain lineage picking their way amid the shattered carcasses of three or four automobiles of indeterminate age, is something that he could attribute only to the inscrutable stupidity of outsiders. Wealth, to a Cherokee, is apt to be understood in terms not of stockpiles against the needs of the future, but of a comforting fulfilment of the requirements of today.

Wealth-getting *idi:gawé:sdi* are generally called

79

tsugv:wahl(o)di ugv:wahli ("wealth/for the purpose of"). Some are lilting poetry per se; others, uncomplicated and childlike, such as this one, are tinged with the simple earnestness of need:

Now! Listen! This is my name: _____.

Little People, from where You rest Above, quickly with
    Your knowledge.

All of You are Wizards: in nothing do You fail.

I ask of You for wealth to become mine.

This is usually implemented by going to running water at daybreak, by saying the charm four times while facing east, and by announcing the name and clan and then washing the face after each complete statement. The ceremony should be performed upon four successive mornings.

The steps necessary to put into full effect the ensuing beautiful *i:gawé:sdi* are carefully spelled out: One goes to a creek or spring at the crack of dawn, faces east, takes tobacco in the palm of the left hand, rolls the tobacco with a counterclockwise motion of the extended fingers of the right hand while singing and saying the charm, after which one spits sharply upon the tobacco and then blows the breath upon it. The ritual is enacted four times. The tobacco thus "remade" one smokes upon venturing out away from home.

M.M. ♩=48 circa

Hu-hu   na- ge- hi   hu- hu- na- ge- hi

hu- hu na- ge- hi   hu- hu na- ge- hi.

Yellow Mockingbird over there! (*sung four times*)

Then You and I will go hunt White Wealth in the night from whence You came.

You are a Wizard as great as the earth is deep.

You fail in nothing.

In the very middle of everywhere on earth where people have wealth, You have just intruded Yourself.

You have done it by witchcraft.
This is my clan, _____, and this is my name _____.

Very quickly You have just brought wealth down to me!

The technique for disseminating the power of the next example is quite similar to that above; the tobacco, however, is not rolled, but placed upon the top of a hat lying near the edge of a stream. One must also be fasting while performing the rite.

Now! Seven Clans of Horseflies! *Ha!* You are great Wizards!

Then very quickly You have just come to apply that, very sweet, which You carry.

You have just flown into the very middle of the diffused Brown Tobacco: You are very wise.

You have just come to apply Your saliva to the Red Tobacco.

Then in the very middle of the wealth of the Seven Clans
    You have just come to make Your home: You have just
    gotten the wealth into Your hand!

This is my name, _____, and this is my clan _____.

You and I have just gotten it all!

    The procedure is again slightly varied when accom-
panying the *i:gawé:sdi* below: while blowing upon the
tobacco, one holds it in outstretched cupped hands up to
the rising sun. Considered as poetry, the text, vibrant in
the original Cherokee with the most delicate and supple
subtleties, is surely a masterpiece of native American
literature.

Now! Listen! *Ha!* On White Pathways I will be making
    my footprints.

There will be no evil: for in front of me Lightning will
    be going, and behind me coming.

For my body, you Seven Clans, is beautified by my
    Provider, and I will fade into this Red Tobacco with
    which I am clothed.

Where the Seven Clans are, I have appeared: I am beau-
    tified. In the very middle of the sunrays I stand; in the
    middle I continue to stand, facing the Sunland.

Now then, you Seven Clans, and those of you who
    founded the Seven Clans, you have wealth near the
    water which I have just come to choose.

You are not to want to keep it: if it can be borrowed, I
    greatly wish to borrow it! Look at me, all of you! My
    name is _____.

"Remaking"
Yú:gwil(a) Root

Mooney[1] identifies the *yú:gwil(a)* plant as Venus' fly-trap (*Dionaea muscipula*); in Mooney and Olbrechts[2] it is identified as pitcher plant (*Sarracenia purpurea*). Both identifications are correct, for the Cherokees themselves speak of two varieties of *yú:gwil(a)*.

The uses that were discovered for *yú:gwil(a)* root in North Carolina — as a fish lure and as an aid to memory (the water collected in the leaf of the pitcher plant was drunk) — have no discernible correlation with the position that it occupies in the culture of the Oklahoma Cherokees. In Oklahoma *yú:gwil(a)* root is considered by the oldsters among the conservatives to be a talisman of well-nigh limitless power, and the fact that it is not indigenous makes it all the more sought after and cherished if obtained.

While there exists a difference of opinion as to whether two *yú:gwil(a)* roots are more powerful than one, the belief that those of red color are more potent than white ones is seemingly universal. But any *yú:gwil(a)* root is valueless as it comes from the ground: it must be "remade," and the technique of "remaking" it is known to but few. So far as we know, all of this root in Oklahoma was sent by friends and relatives in North Carolina, or else was obtained by some Western Cherokee visiting at Qualla.

Since *yú:gwil(a)* is so precious, only very small sections of it — a half-inch to two inches or so in length — are "remade" and kept. If anything, *yú:gwil(a)* is more sensitive than is "remade" tobacco to influences that might break its power; therefore, it is not kept inside a home. It is put into a small bag of soft deerskin and placed in some such location as upon a rafter of a porch, or in a shed or barn. It is strongly believed by many individuals that "remade" *yú:gwil(a)* roots will of their own volition move away from something that imperils their power, and for that reason they cannot always be found in the exact spot in which they were placed.

A person transfers to himself the magical qualities of "remade" *yú:gwil(a)* by rubbing the bag in which it is contained upon his hands, and then passing his hands over his face and body. Such action is taken when leaving home upon some mission, the success of which he wishes to guarantee.

Yú:gwil(a) can be invested with its magical powers either at dawn or at night. If the conjurer elects to "work" at daybreak, he places the *yú:gwil(a)* in the palm of his right hand as he faces east by a stream, dips it underwater while still holding the palm upward, says an *i:gawé:sdi* four times, and blows his breath upon the root after each recitation.

This text is much used for the above purpose:

You White Man! You rest in the Sunland.

Provider, You have just come to hear. You have just come to "remake" for me the White Medicine. It is the medicine of the Seven Clans.

At peace I live in the distant Sunrays. My name is

————.

The Sun follows His Clan with His Eye. As much as is the Sun, I am covered with the Word.

All of Your Pathways have just come to turn: they will be burrowing under my soul. Your Pathways will never end.

I am attired like the White Swan. White Swan, all about I will be commanding.

The Eyes of a Person will be in my body, never to glance away.

A ceremony for "remaking" *yú:gwil(a)* at night is always enacted at the time of the new moon. The conjurer faces east near running water upon which moonlight is shining; while holding the root in the palm of his left hand, he dips the forefinger of his right hand into the water and with this finger gently moistens the *yú:gwil(a)*. He then says the following four times and blows his breath upon the root after each statement. At this juncture he decides upon what specific purpose the talisman is to serve (to gain wealth, to insure good luck in gambling, etc.).

Now! Listen! Red Moon! Quickly You have just emerged, attired in Red.

Quickly You have just come to lend me Your Red Attire: then I will not be attired in loneliness.

The Eyes of the Seven Corners will continually be in my body: I will be finding the Taker[3] in the Seven Corners.

They will intend the Taker to be for Beads: I will burrow under the White House; I am not to meet the Taker.

Yú:gwil(a) was told that He and I are great Wizards: He
and I have just come to live with all of those in the
Clan Districts.

It is evident that They have just brought the Taker. My
(Seven!)[4] Attire they have just come to snatch away.

This is the way it happened. Seven!

Since both *yú:gwil(a)* and Adam-and-Eve roots are difficult to procure, sometimes a silver dollar is "remade" in
substitution by means of the method we have just
described.

For *"Cleaning" Yú:gwil(a) Root Defiled by a "Door-Closer"*

The power of *yú:gwil(a)* root is not permanently lost
when broken by what is called *ul(i)sdu:dhanó:hi* ("it
closed him [or her] out") — the touch or presence of a
menstrual or pregnant woman, a corpse, or someone who
has been in contact with, or in the vicinity of, a corpse.
It can be "cleaned" by going to running water at daybreak, facing the rising sun, holding the *yú:gwil(a)* in the
right hand and saying the following four times, and after
each recitation dipping it with an underhand motion into
the stream and then blowing the breath upon it. One
enactment of this ritual is actually sufficient, but to perform it upon four successive mornings is considered to be
strengthening.
    The *i:gawé:sdi* is this:

Long Man,[5] You have been designated Protector.

You were designated to be cleaning it of the Blue who,
   bent down, is burrowing in and out.

You who were informed, very quickly You have just come
   over here to clean us.

You have just come to put my soul Over There!

"Remaking"
Adam-and-Eve Roots

The roots of the Adam-and-Eve plant (*Aplectrum
hyemale*) are sometimes accepted as a substitute for
yú:gwil(a). They, too, must be "remade." Adam-and-Eve
must long have been considered to have had magical
qualities, for Mooney[6] states that a deer hunter of his
day inserted a small piece of the chewed root of the plant
into the wound that killed a deer, ". . . expecting as a
necessary result to find the animal unusually fat when
skinned." He also mentions that infants were bathed in
a decoction of the root for the purpose of fattening them.

The extension of "to make fat" to embrace "to make
wealthy" is a logical one. Adam-and-Eve roots are especially prized for their wealth-getting properties, and it
is customary to keep them in the natural environment of
whatever it is that one wishes to acquire: i.e., if household furnishings are desired, the root is kept in the house;
if livestock is the goal, in the barn. "Remade" Adam-and-
Eve is susceptible to the same malign influences that
break the power of "remade" tobacco and *yú:gwil(a)*.

It is widely held that the Adam-and-Eve plant will not
live near white men, but will "leave" a vicinity into which
they move. There is a sound scientific basis for this con-

cept. The plant is a delicate one that requires undis-
turbed leaf mold. The livestock of the whites, who are
primarily stockmen, destroy the plant's environmental
necessities. It has become exceedingly rare in Oklahoma
Cherokeeia.

Not only are Adam-and-Eve roots "remade" with a
procedure similar to that employed in "remaking" *yu:-
gwil(a)*, but the wording of the *i:gawé:sdi* is likely to be
nearly the same:

Now! You White Man![7] You rest toward the Sunland.

You Provider, You have just come to hear. You have
just come to "remake" for me the White Medicine. It
is the Medicine for the Seven Clans.

In the very middle of the treetops I stand. Adam-and-
Eve, my name is ————, my clan is ————.

The Sun is not[8] to follow with His Eye. As much as is the
Sun, I am covered with the Word.

All of your Pathways have just come to turn: they will
not[9] be burrowing under my soul.

I am attired like the White Swan. White Swan, all about
I will be commanding.

The Eyes of a Person will be in my body, never to glance
away from my body.

IX

Games and Gaming

Games and Gaming   IX

Cornstalk-Shooting

OTHER THAN upon ceremonial occasions, the ancient sport of cornstalk-shooting is not much in evidence these days; but up until about a generation ago it flourished as an expression of the competitive spirit of the individual Cherokee community. A cornstalk-shooting might be held at any time of the year, although warm weather for the occasion was considered highly desirable. Each team had the services of a conjurer from the community it represented who "worked" for its success the night preceding the contest. Prizes of as much as $200, or perhaps a cow, were awarded the winning team of twenty archers.

There were no specifications as to the length or the lay

of the field upon which the competition was held. At each end of it there was constructed a rack about two feet high, two feet long, and two feet thick, into which two hundred dry cornstalks were placed. One team used arrows that were painted red; the arrows of the opposing team were unpainted. The length of the arrows was subject to no regulation.

One team lined up at a predetermined distance facing, but slightly to the right of, one of the racks; the other team took a corresponding position to the left. The first archer of Team A then discharged his arrow at the rack of cornstalks; he was followed by the first member of Team B. After all forty men had thus alternatively shot, an examination was made to ascertain if either the red or the plain arrows had penetrated as many as 150 cornstalks, the prescribed number for victory. If there was no winner, both teams (without walking upon the field itself and thus violating some antique taboo) repaired to the opposite end of the field and shot a round at the other rack. This usually determined victory.

In view of the fact that the prize, at least by Cherokee economic standards, was not inconsiderable, it is not surprising that some of the players had a few tricks up their quivers to enhance their chance of winning. Some carried seven splinters of lightning-struck wood in their pockets. Some knew an *i:gawé:sdi* or two. Some knew a little ritual wherein the archer placed his arrow in his bow, said the following once, then put the first and second fingers of his right hand to his mouth and obtained a bit of saliva which he applied to the point and nock of his arrow:

Listen! Black Spider, quickly You have just come to pull the arrow out of its quiver.

Shooter! Shooter! Shooter! Shooter!

While an archer was undoubtedly primarily interested in the success of his own shot, nevertheless he gave some thought to insuring the failure of that of his opponent. He therefore said this four times, blowing his breath toward his adversary after each statement:

Listen! From over there the Buzzard tells that He has just come and brushed aside your aim with His wings.

Then your soul is turned! *Hayi:! Dayi:!*

Ballplaying

While no exhaustive study of the ball game called by the Cherokees *a:nalá:sgali:sgó* ("repeatedly they are putting it into the mouth") has yet been published, the literature is rich in passing comments upon it and brief descriptions of it.[1] Except for infrequent and rather self-conscious contests slightly tinged with tourism, staged upon ceremonial occasions, it is all but extinct in Oklahoma.

A good many charms used in playing this game have survived, however. One of them is to "remake" tobacco to be quickly chewed and spit upon the field where opposing players are likely to come in contact with it:

Now! Red Lightning! *Ha!* Very quickly You have just come to strike with Red Sticks!

Ha! Very quickly You have just come to knock off the hands of the Seven Peoples!

And there is a counter-charm to nullify the magic of opponents, used in "remaking" tobacco, the smoke of which its reciter blows upon himself four times:

Now! Listen! Fishinghawk, You are a Great Wizard! You and I have just come to unite in friendship.

Now! This, then, is my name, _____. I have just come to "remake" myself.

Now! Fishinghawk, You are a Wizard! Now completely appear.

Brown Tobacco, You are a Great Wizard! You have just come to strike their hearts!

Gambling

There is very little in ethnographic literature and even less in tribal oral tradition that would give an indication as to whether the Cherokees were, in aboriginal times, more addicted to gambling than other North American Indians, or whether they were less so. We know that they gambled[2] — sometimes by methods that have been sketchily reported or not reported at all.

Certainly their favorite game of chance these days is the white man's poker, which they play with uncommon cunning and skill. Gambling techniques that require little intellectual effort, such as rolling dice, hold little attraction. But not all poker players are willing to trust entirely to ability and luck. There exists a class of *idi:gawé:sdi* for the purpose of providing a little additional help. They are called by the generic term *di:ghwaniyosdí:i* ("to gamble, one").

Some of these are said (or thought) prior to beginning a game, or at any critical juncture during the course of a game. They are usually quite brief and, of course, are delivered four times. Fairly typical is:

Red Lightning! Very quickly You have just come to strike.

You were not empty-handed: the wealth that I asked You for became more beautiful!

Most gambling *idi:gawé:sdi* are for "remaking" chewing tobacco. In the conventional manner, it is taken at dawn to the presence of running water and, while facing east, the conjurer recites an appropriate text over it four times and spits and blows his breath upon it following each recitation. A bit of it is chewed during a card game, and a minute amount of the tobacco juice is surreptitiously expectorated upon the hands or used to wet the fingers.

The resemblance between this spell for "remaking" chewing tobacco for use while gambling and a typical *tsugv́:wahl(o)di ugv:wahli i:gawé:sdi* is understandable, for both are for acquiring something valuable:

Now! Sparrow Hawk!

Very quickly You have just descended to me.

In the very middle of the wealth of the Seven Clan Districts You have just alighted.

You have taken all of it: it has become Yours.

Now then! My name is _____; my clan is _____.

White Eagle, You have approved of it.

You have just turned over all the wealth to me!

In the succeeding *i:gawé:sdi* the gambling stakes, the "White Medicine," are identified by name. The gambler assures himself that he, too, is "remade" and invested with the power of Thunder, "the One who lives on the Other Side of the Mountain":

Now! Listen! You rest Above, Red Man!

Now! *Ha!* Quickly, White Medicine. It is _____.

You have an overabundance of wealth that You have just come to put into my lap.

As high as the treetops He will be walking, the One who lives on the Other Side of the Mountain.

I have just come to pull away the White Medicine.

I, _____, have just come to "remake" myself.

I am a Red Man!

The "Important Thing" mentioned in this prayer, which in the original language rings with literary quality, is a circumlocution for evil, failure, disaster. The term is much used in curing conjurations wherein it represents disease, or a manifestation of a disease.

Now! Listen! My Provider! Now! Now I have just inquired of You.

I have just come to lift up my soul. My Provider, You have permitted me to do it.

Ha! Now I have just come to remake my heart: I have just come to lift it up.

I will lift it up: the Important Thing cannot climb over
me.

I will gather wealth quietly, *Dhla:nuwa:* Your Saliva
walks Above.

I inquired of You: "Do You think it is good?"

I stand as bright as the Sunburst!

X

Courts and Law Enforcement

Courts and Law Enforcement

Influencing Courts

THE BENCH and the bar in eastern Oklahoma — many positions upon which are ably filled by Cherokees, who have a positive flair for the legal profession — have a tendency to regard cases involving Cherokees, especially those concerning Cherokees versus Cherokees, as proverbially slippery and difficult to try. Cherokees agree, and smile knowingly. For they have *idi:gawé:sdi* that are said (or merely thought), or used to "remake" tobacco, that operate to weary judges, to create indecision in juries, to raise dissension in the prosecuting team, and to addle witnesses. These spells are potent magic indeed, and highly secret.

One *i:gawé:sdi* of special value in a case concerning

a rather minor criminal offense is this one, said but once outside the courtroom by a friend or relative of the defendant. The speaker then comes to the doorway and attracts the attention of the participants in the trial by some such ruse as clearing his throat or shuffling his feet, thus propelling the power of the incantation toward those for whom it was intended.

Now! I am going to where the Toads are chattering.

What are They discussing?

Someone charged with a crime as serious as that of homicide can be assisted by means as simple as an *i:gawé:sdi* and an attention-getting maneuver. This following specimen, to help a person charged with murder or manslaughter, is not said aloud: it is thought four times. The accused may already have done what he could for himself by having drunk water, for thirty days or so prior to the trial, from a glass in which he had placed a bullet that he had found somewhere.

Now! Fishinghawk!

Ha! Very quickly You have just come down to the very middle of the Thicket.

You have just come to give him life.

Then You great Wizard, You can fail in nothing!

Now this is his name, _____, and this is his clan, _____.

You have just come to raise up his soul.

You released him alive!

The "Thicket" into which the powerful and resourceful bird spirit has descended may be a metaphor for the difficulties with which the beneficiary of this spell is surrounded.

There is a spell to "remake" tobacco to aid a defendant that is itself short, but the ritual in which it is used is time-consuming. The sorcerer goes at midnight to running water, sings the song and recites the spoken part of the incantation four times, washes his face, throws water over his head seven times, then rolls the tobacco (cut twist). This ritual is enacted three more times during the course of the night. The occasions are so spaced as to permit the last one to occur just as dawn is beginning to break. The sorcerer fasts throughout the entire ensuing day. The tobacco thus "remade" is smoked in or in the vicinity of the courtroom by both the defendant and the sorcerer.

This is the spell:

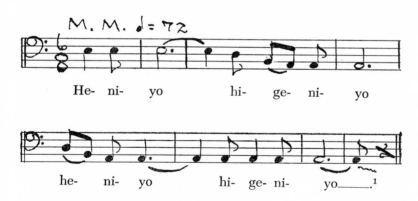

He- ni- yo   hi- ge- ni- yo

he- ni- yo   hi- ge- ni- yo____.[1]

My soul is not to return.

The Little Person is not to return.

The Wizard is not to return.

Now! Listen! At night their feet will be pointed toward the Seven Clans, never to be traced!

The meaning of the text appears to be: "My soul, as powerful as that Wizard, a Little Person, will be released from its difficulty, never to return to it. My enemies will just wander off into the night, and no one will ever know what became of them."

An *i:gawé:sdi* to "remake" tobacco for the express purpose of confusing witnesses in a trial, found written in a small Adair County medicine book, carries a footnote stating that one should "work" beside bubbling water:

I climbed over the Seven Clans. To the middle of your bodies I carry earth: I am not to move.

Ha! My soul travels upon the treetops!

Now! *Ha!* Your hearts are filled with bells.

Your hearts are filled with sand.

Your hearts are filled with stone.

Your hearts are filled with earth.

Ha! It was possible to muzzle him, and one could speak for him!

So?! So?! So?! So?![2]

*Assisting Prisoners
To Escape*

There exist *idi:gawé:sdi* for the express purpose of aiding prisoners in regaining their freedom. Examples of

them are extremely difficult to obtain, for apparently
they are few in number and known but to few.

The two specimens presented here are patently cog-
nates; the one, however, is for the use of someone interested in helping a prisoner escape, while the other is for
the prisoner himself to use. Since both of these examples
refer to the "White Wolf-places" (*loci* of the Wolf Clan?)
as the scene of the prisoner's origin, there is a strong
probability that the incantations were originally the ex-
clusive possessions of the Wolf Clan people. We know,
however, that they are considered to be of efficacy in a
situation involving a member of any clan.

If circumstances permit, the individual employing the
incantation below goes at dawn to live water, faces east,
and delivers the song and the saying four times. After
its statement he laves his face and throws water over his
head seven times. If the "going to the water" must be
omitted, the spell is merely sung and said four times
toward the place where the prisoner is confined.

I came from the White Wolf-places.

Now! I came from the dens in the Wolf-places: I came
from the White Wolf-places.

I came from the Little Wolf-places.

Now! Your souls in the Seven Clan Districts have been
deeply buried!

If in the remote past the foregoing incantation was
used for the benefit of a captive taken in intertribal war,
and it very likely was so employed, then the allusion to
victory over Cherokee clans would appear to be inappro-
priate; but in any *i:gawé:sdi* the terms "Seven Clans" and
"Seven Clan Districts" may be interpreted as metaphors
for "mankind" and "the whole world."

The *"Woduhi"* of the previous spell and the *"Duhi"* of
the following one, to be delivered four times by the
prisoner himself, are, to be sure, Wolf-calls; however,
they are not meaningless vocalizations, but contractions
of the word *uwo:du:hiyu* ("very beautiful, it").

Duhi! (*sung four times*)
I came from the middle of the Rock-places.

Duhi! (*sung four times*)
I came from the Little Rock-places.

Duhi! (*sung four times*)
I came from the Little White Wolf-places.

Their souls from our Clan Districts have been buried
over there!

This is the tune:

hi____ du- hi____.

Aiding Fugitives
From the Law

Undoubtedly there exist a sizable number of charms for assisting persons accused of crime in their efforts to avoid capture, but seldom is one of these to be found written down. An example, carefully penciled in a well-preserved stationery tablet that came from the vicinity of Sugar Mountain at the northern end of Tenkiller Lake, is especially interesting, for its label reads: "This is to use to make officers of the law forget and to hide from them (merely to be said), and also to help in a wrong against the people if they fight back."

Nearly the whole of the Cherokee attitude toward law is expressed or implied here: one violates a law in the legitimate expression of, or in the defense of, one's natural rights; therefore, the law is at fault, not its violator. Since it is the law that commits a "wrong against the people," its violator is entitled to all the assistance he can get, supernatural or otherwise. One is easily persuaded that if a medieval seigneur had had Cherokee serfs, he would have had to contend with a Jacquerie every day of his life — for however long that would have been.

The text of the Sugar Mountain charm is simply this:

Black Yellow Mockingbird!

Your lonely souls are confused!

Protecting and Aiding
Peace Officers

Outlawry in the Cherokee Hills has found its histo-
rians, literary and oral. Most have thoroughly misunder-
stood what they reported. The Cherokees have no
weakness for homicide: their chief failing is a touchiness
in a fantastic degree on the question of their rights. The
lawlessness that marred the pages of Cherokee history
for a century after the Removal is not a testimony to any
innate love of bloodshed in Cherokees, but rather to their
astonishing ability to prolong a subterranean civil war
that had its root in the question of whether or not to
collaborate with the white man.

The white man who forced them from their homes in
the Southeast set the stage for intramural bloodshed in
the West. But he very obligingly did more than that: he
stoked the fire that he had kindled. The jagged and roadless hills of the Cherokee Nation provided refuge for the
wanted (and the unwanted) from the United States who
added their guns to those of the Indian factions or went
into business for themselves. Even as late as the days of
the Great Depression, bank robbers and metropolitan
gangsters made frequent use of the caves and coves of
the Cherokee hills.

In the old Cherokee Nation each district had law
enforcement machinery guided by an elected official
called a *di:daʔni·yí:sgi* ("one who apprehends them").
His life was an adventurous one, and sometimes short.
Many of the notorious scofflaws were master conjurers
as well as excellent marksmen. It paid any peace officer

dealing with the likes of these to be as knowing in his magic as in his shooting.

Some manhunters were probably medicine men themselves, and knew how to get the conjuring drop on their quarries. If they were not, they could go to some good law-loving sorcerer who would "remake" tobacco for them to moisten and rub upon their bodies or to smoke toward the concealed outlaws.

Here are four *idi:gawé:sdi* exclusively for "remaking" tobacco designed to strengthen the arm of the law:

1.

Now! Little Wolves! Very quickly all of You bark so that nothing can climb over.

They cross your Path at the treetops.

Now! Big Wolves! They just come trailing you.

Now! "They will corner you right now in the Wolf-places," I will be saying.

2.

Now! Listen! The Seven Thunderers[3] will be watching out in front of me as I go. *Ha,* then! My attire will be most terrifying!

Now! Seven Kinds of People! *Ha,* then! Now they will not be able to climb over me.

Now! They will be tying the legs of the Sleepy Red Deer[4] in front of me as I go.

This is my clan, _____, my name, _____.

3.

Now! Black Spider! Now very quickly You and I have just come to cut off his legs!

Now! Then very secretly You and I have just crawled up to Those-Who-Take.

You and I will be crawling upon their backs.

Ha, then! They[5] have just cut off their[6] legs!

The Seven Kinds of People are not to find it out.

Now! Black Dog! I will be standing about![7]

My clan is _____, my name is _____.

4.

Now! Screech Owl! Here! Here! Here! Here!

You are a great Wizard!

Always in the middle of the night You pass by.

Now! Brown Screech Owl! Very quickly You have just come to put the White Ancient Tobacco in my pipe.

Now! Brown Screech Owl! (*Ha!* He overcame it!) You are a great Wizard!

Now You and I have just come to lift up the White Smoke.

You and I have just come to extract the souls of the Seven Those-Who-Take![8]

XI

Divining

DiviningXI

Divining by
Various Means

DIVINING occupies a salient place in Cherokee society. It is practiced in various modes, for diverse ends — and it is practiced much. Some of the principal methods of divining are: by means of a plummet or silver coin suspended upon a string or thong; by means of small, nugget-like stones, or seed beads, held in the hands; by means of needles (or the aforementioned beads) set afloat in a bowl, or small hole, of water; by means of controlled dreams; and by means of a stick partially immersed in a stream.

Some of the chief reasons for engaging a diviner are: to determine the cause and prognosis of an illness; to inquire into life expectancy; to learn if one is being

113

molested, or is about to be molested, by a witch; and to ascertain the whereabouts of a missing mate, estrayed farm animals, or lost or stolen possessions.

Any *dida:hnvwi:sg(i)* is prepared to supply a divining service, but there also exist specialists in the field of clairvoyance. A diviner of repute may be given to carrying some of the tools of his trade in his pocket so as to be prepared for a sudden demand upon his talent.

Perhaps the commonest mode of divining in matters of no very great moment is with a plummet. Some practitioners use a silver coin instead of a lump of lead; others consider a gold coin, or artifact of gold, to be superior to silver. In any case, the implement must be of some material that "comes from the ground." In the event that a silver coin is employed, it is donated by the client and retained by the diviner as the *u:gi:sdi*, the gift of the essence of oneself to which illness or evil or doubt is symbolically transferred. The suspended object is allowed to move freely in the air, or else it is barely immersed in a new bowl, or perhaps a creekside hole of water the approximate size of a bowl, and answers are supplied by the direction in which the object moves. East, of course, is the "fortunate" or "positive" direction in all matters to which these qualities are applicable.

One of the *idi:gawé:sdi* employed in divining with a piece of metal in water is this simple and noble prayer:

You Provider! You rest on high.

In Your Hand the body of a person is shortened,[1] and
　You make everything here on the surface of the earth.

Now very quickly I have just come to let You know.

Now I will be hearing what You state.

Now very quickly I have just come to inquire of You.

My name is _____.

You Ancient White One! Now You will tell me the truth.

This is recited four times previous to immersing the divining implement.

In divining by means of stones, two pebbles approximately the size of acorns are tightly clenched, one in each hand. An *i:gawé:sdi* such as the following is said four times. Then the diviner opens his hands and carefully observes the stones: if the one in the right hand moves, the answer is favorable; if the one in the left hand moves, there is bad news for the client.

Beads, two white ones in the right hand and two black ones in the left hand, can be used in place of stones, and they are so used with the ensuing, an *i:gawé:sdi* specifically employed to locate something lost:

Listen! *Ha!* You Two Little Men![2]

Ha! You Two overlook nothing.

Ha! It is tracked down on the Pathway: You Two are knowing; You Two are great Wizards.

Ha! In the resting place of Wizards on high—*Ha!*—You Two overlook nothing.

Ha! It is tracked down on the Pathway.

Ha! On the Pathway You Two are lying nearby the Quarry.

Ha! Over there your soul, which is the Red Quarry, just rose up!

Divining with needles is much resorted to by
din(a)da:hnvwi:sg(i)[3] for the purpose of appraising the
gravity of the illness of a client. Although a bowl of water
may be used indoors, a small creekside pothole is deemed
to be even better. Whichever may be used, at daybreak
the diviner places two needles in the palm of his hand,
recites an *i:gawé:sdi* such as the following, and blows
upon the needles. The reciting and the blowing of the
breath are done, of course, a total of four times. One of
the needles, balanced upon the middle finger of the right
hand, is set afloat; resting upon the middle finger of the
left hand, the other needle is then placed in the water
at a distance of about four inches if a bowl is being used,
at about a foot if a hole of water is being employed. If
the lefthand needle drifts over (headfirst is especially
ominous) and touches its companion, a poor prognosis
is obtained; if the sinistral needle strikes the dextral one
in such a manner as to cause the latter to founder, the
conclusion is that only the most extraordinary efforts can
save the patient. If, however, the needles keep their distance or float even farther apart, the outlook is hopeful.

This is a typical *i:gawé:sdi* used in needle-divining:

> You Provider!
>
> I ask You.
>
> You know.
>
> Tell me the way it is.

A pair of beads, the one on the right white, the other
black, can be used similarly. Here is an *i:gawé:sdi* specifically for divining with floating beads:

Listen! Now You and I have just come to bring the Red
   Beads together. [*The beads are placed in the water.*]

The Blue cannot do it.

I have just placed them upon the Pathway.

They are very quick. Listen!

The best method of divination by water for medical
reasons, but one that requires consummate mastery in
interpreting the findings, is that by means of a newly cut
stick about two or three feet long. The kind of tree from
which the stick is cut, strangely enough, is of no conse-
quence. The diviner, alone at the edge of a stream at
daybreak, faces the reddening east, moistens one end of
the stick in his mouth, and states his name and the name
of his patient (the clans of both may be optionally added). He then puts the stick, the unmoistened end downward, into the water deep enough to immerse the stick
for approximately half of its length, and slowly describes
with it four counterclockwise circles about two feet in
diameter, timing each revolution so that it will be syn-
chronous with one full statement of the prayer below.
He then brings the stick to the center of the circle, lets
it rest there briefly, and studies the appearance of the
water within the compass of the circle.

If a crayfish or a minnow from deeper water or an
insect from the bank darts into the delineated area, and
especially should one of these creatures investigate the
stick, such is accepted as proof that the patient has been
made ill by sorcery. If during the diviner's examination
a bird should fly overhead and call out, such an occurrence also points conclusively to the fact that doctor and

patient have to deal with witchcraft. Floating debris of any kind is a bad omen, and the floating in of a dead leaf is a portent of certain death. But quite clear water is also a sinister omen: the patient, if not already dead, is doomed. A certain amount of aimless activity, such as a single object leisurely moving in the water, is what the diviner hopes to see; for in that case the patient will recover.

Now! Long Person, I have just come to pray to You.

Wahhya hi:nadu! (sung four times)

Now! You will "remake" my soul.

It will become longer.

I will rise again.

Wahhya hi:nadu! (sung four times)

I will be greeting You with my soul!

The melody is:

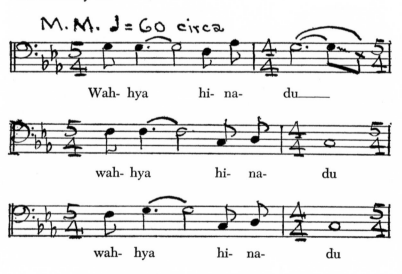

wah- hya   hi- na-   du_____.

Wahhya is the word for wolf: the wolf is a symbol of wizardry; *Hi:nadu:!* is the voice of Thunder.

A dream is sometimes employed in divining. While a dream is of value in acquiring information of any sort, it is considered to be particularly efficacious in determining whether or not a relative or friend is being conjured. The diviner merely announces upon retiring that he wishes to ascertain something in particular, and then before dropping off to sleep thinks, but does not say, the prayer below. He must remain mute until morning in order to get the full benefit of his dreaming. If his dream is difficult for him to interpret, he may seek the advice of another diviner.

Now! Listen! I am the doer of Your Will: You love me, You Ancient Red One!

I say to You, "Your Food!"

You possess me overnight: I am filled with life.

Nothing can alight upon me.

Freely let me be turning over and over: I have appeared like the Water Strider.

Ha! I have to finish that which I am keeping.

I am _____.

In everyday language this prayer might read:

May I have Your attention now? Thunder, I obey You, and You love me for it.

You feed upon my soul.

All night long I am filled with Your Spirit, which is life itself.

No evil can come to me.

Make my consciousness weightless and free, like the movements of that agile insect, the Water Strider.

Well! You know I have a duty to perform: to find out something.

You know me; for I am _____.

Finding Lost
Livestock

In terms of the economy of the white world, the Cherokee's livestock constitutes his most valuable possession. Since up until quite recently in Oklahoma Cherokeeia the open range principle was generally adhered to, his horses, cattle, and hogs wandered at will in the wilderness, and they frequently became lost, and not infrequently were stolen.

There are divining *idi:gawé:sdi* for the express purpose of locating missing livestock. One example, seen in a medicine book dating from the 1880's, states that it is for finding a lost horse, that a suspended plummet should be used, and that one should say the prayer four times. An *i:gawé:sdi* of this type can be used anywhere, at any time of day. The lead moves in the direction of the missing animal.

Now! Provider!

I have just come to inquire of You.

> This, ————, is its name.
>
> You will show me the direction.

There is another prayer that is available for finding any kind of livestock. The divining implement generally employed with it is a half dollar, suspended like a plummet.

> Now! Provider, You are the Ruler of Heaven and the earth, and You are not unfamiliar with the life and utterance of everything here on earth.
>
> Now! You will now inform me as to exactly where it is, and indicate to me if it yet lives.
>
> You and I will hunt it, and You will also let me hear.

XII

Revenge

Revenge **XII**

Producing Misfortune
And Death

THE NORTH CAROLINA Cherokee rituals to achieve revenge[1] tend toward the formal, the circumlocutory and
complex; in Oklahoma they are characteristically simple,
short, and blazing with elementary venom. Seldom will
anyone admit that he ever saw or heard one of the grisly
incantations, not to mention confess to knowing one. If
they are to be found written, they are usually captioned
in some such vague fashion as "to lower his soul."

This example is for heaping upon a personal enemy
any misfortune whatever that the user of it wishes, up
to and including death in the most gruesome of forms.
The conjurer "remakes" tobacco with it for four successive mornings. If he decides that his enemy is to die, he

fasts the entire last day of his "working." In the usual manner, the smoke of the tobacco is blown directly upon the victim, if possible, or otherwise in his general direction.

This is what is said:

Now! Listen! *Ha!* Now very quickly You have just swooped down, Blue Sparrow Hawk! You rest Above.

You are to take the Blue Tobacco. *Ha!* The Blue Tobacco has just come to inform you, _____!

Ha! He leaped from Up There and has just appeared down here. *Ha!* The Pathway has just sloped down from Above.

These are their names, _____. In the very middle of their Places of Repose You have just come to whoop!

We have just come to make utterly miserable the souls of _____. The Blue Tobacco has just come to lay them underground.

Ha! He has just come to examine their souls. In the very middle of my breast where they have just come to live, You have just come to take their lives!

Now! I stand in the Sunland: I am entirely Red. I am not lonely in the Clan Districts.

With this shorter but no less terrible incantation, *tso:-lagayb:li,* mixed with ordinary tobacco, is customarily used:

Red Thunder! Very quickly You have just come to clutch the souls of people.

Red Mountain Lion! Quickly You have just come to live with them.

You and I have just come to wake the souls in the Nightland.

Let the Black live with all of you forever!

Producing Insanity

Some revenge-getting *idi:gawé:sdi* are used for a restricted purpose which is indicated by the wording, as is the case of this one for making an enemy insane. It does not require tobacco for its dissemination: one merely states the name and clan of the victim, delivers the incantation four times, and then blows one's breath toward him after each rendition:

Your Pathways are Black: it was wood, not a human being![2]

Dog excrement will cling nastily to you.

You will be living intermittently. "*Wo?!*"[3] You will be saying along toward the Nightland.

Your Black Viscera will be lying all about. You will be lonely.

You will be like the Brown Dog in heat. You are changed: you have just become old. This is your clan _____.

In the very middle of the Prairie, changed, you will be carrying dog stools. "*Wo?!*" you will be saying.

Your Pathway lies toward the Nightland!

XIII

War and Strife

War and Strife　　　XIII

War

THE QUANTITY of surviving *idi:gawé:sdi* pertaining to war is somewhat surprising in view of the fact that the Cherokees, flying in the face of expert ethnological opinion, do not consider themselves ever to have been particularly warlike, and are given to disparaging somewhat the tribes that were. The clue may be found in the white military headstones sown across the green Cherokee Hills, for one sometimes gets the impression that the white man's burden at the ends of empire has been borne by disproportionately few white men.

However full may be the ceremonies designed to protect a soldier going away to war, whatever service he can do for himself in the blaze of battle is understandably brief. Most battle *idi:gawé:sdi* are quite short. But oddly enough, so is one, stated below, for making *wo:di,* or war paint; for the preparation of this protective took a considerable amount of time.

In the old days war paint was made from a variety of substances selected for diverse reasons: from some sort of sweet-smelling fungus; from a gland in the throat of a lizard; from a species of butterfly that "flies fast" and would therefore confer agility upon the wearer of *wo:di* made from it; and from hematite, especially prized because it is found "inside stone," and "one cannot shoot through stone." The paint-maker went at dawn to the most secluded spot he knew to do his work. He said the following four times over his handiwork, blew his breath upon it, and held it up to the rising sun after each recitation. He fasted all day after completing his task.

You Little Red Man! *Ho:!*[1] Quickly we have just met!

You Little Black Man! *Ho:!* Quickly we have just met!

You Little Yellow Man! *Ho:!* Quickly we have just met!

You Little White Man! *Ho:!* Quickly we have just met!

One of the shortest *idi:gawé:sdi* that we have encountered comes from an individual who saw action in World War II. He is strongly of the opinion that it simultaneously shielded him from danger and discomfited the enemy to whom it was said:

You Wizards! I am as much a Wizard as You!

Certain war-charms are for the express purpose of protection against "bullets" (*gaʔni,* the ancient word for arrows, is used for the white man's bullets). After saying

this one the soldier spits upon his hands and then symbolically "goes to the water" by applying the saliva to his
face, chest, and such other parts of the body as the occasion will permit. The *i·gawé·sdi* is said and the ritual
performed a total of four times. The same charm is also
sometimes used when one stands in danger of becoming
embroiled in a fight, or even as an emergency measure
against a *dida·hnese·sg(i)*.

Listen! You Two Little Men Above![2]

Now very quickly You have just come down from the
Sunland.

Right now the One who knows me will lift Himself up.

Dayi·!

The "*Dayi·!*" represents the sound of a missile in flight.
An example of another type of charm for fighting men
carries this footnote: "To hide from them when you are
surprised by an ambush on the road, for a *ga?ni* not to
hit you, and to help you in war." It stands midway between a "to help me in war" and a "to hide with" charm.
Seemingly it is to be said but once.

Red Lightning! *Ha!* You will be holding my soul in Your
clenched Hand.

Ha! As high as the Red Treetops—*Ha!*—my soul will be
alive and moving over there.

Ha! It will be glimmering here below.

Ha! My body will become the size of a hair, the size of
my shadow!

Fighting

Charms to assist and to protect an individual in an altercation of some sort constitute a genre distinct from war *idi:gawé:sdi,* but the two types are, of course, to some degree interchangeable. Fighting charms are not uniformly labeled, but they are likely to be given some such title as *a:nahlihʌ́:i ahl(i)sdé:hl(v)doʔdí* ("fighting, they/to help one with, it"). Like the war charms, ordinarily they are said four times, and they are followed by a similar token "going to the water" with saliva, but sometimes tobacco is "remade" with them.

One of them goes thus:

Da:hl(a)! Da:hl(a)! Da:hl(a)! Da:hl(a)![3]

Now! Blue Lightning! You have just come to slap the earth in front of the warring.

Now Thunder has just come to stamp in front of the Seven Clan Districts and the Seven Peoples.

Put their souls down upon the ground!

Another one reads:

1.

Diamondback Rattlesnake! Right here You rest.

You and I are friends.

Make a clash in the very middle of my body!

Let them be terrified of me!

2.

Ugh(a)dhe:n(i)! Right here You rest.

You and I are friends.

Make a clash in the very middle of my body!

Ha! Let them be terrified of me!

3.

Red Mountain Lion! Right here You rest.

You and I are friends.

Make a clash in the very middle of my body!

Ha! Let them be terrified of me!

This is used for "remaking" tobacco in anticipation of the possibility of a fight. The smoke of the tobacco serves to intimidate prospective challengers.

Another example, written here with the slight alterations in the repetitions indicated, is used with saliva, as mentioned above:

1.

Now! Listen! The jaws of the Diamondback Rattlesnake hang in the very middle of my breast!

Now! Listen! The jaws of the Red Mountain Lion fill all the space in the very middle of my breast!

Then I have climbed over the Seven Clans!

This, then is my clan, _____.

2.

Now! Listen! The jaws of the *Ugh(a)dhe:n(a)* hang in the very middle of my breast!

Now! Listen! The jaws of the Red Mountain Lion fill all the space in the very middle of my breast!

Then I have climbed over the Seven Clans!

This, then, is my clan, _____.

3.

Now! Listen! The jaws of the Blacksnake hang in the very middle of my breast!

Now! Listen! The jaws of the Red Mountain Lion fill all the space in the very middle of my breast!

Then I have climbed over the Seven Clans!

This, then, is my clan, _____.

4.

Now! Listen! The jaws of the Velvettail Rattlesnake hang in the very middle of my breast!

Now! Listen! The jaws of the Red Mountain Lion fill all the space in the very middle of my breast!

Then I have climbed over the Seven Clans!

This, then, is my clan, _____.[4]

XIV

Forgetting and Remembering

Forgetting and Remembering **XIV**

Inducing Forgetfulness

CHEROKEES ARE exceedingly circumspect in meeting strangers — especially Cherokee strangers. They are careful not to offend by the word or deed that might be misinterpreted as hostility; for there is the ever-present danger that the visitor might resort to witchcraft to avenge a fancied slight or insult. Silence, not forced small talk, is the proper climate for solidifying social cement; the jest is an embossed invitation to trouble.

Cherokees, who can be the most implacable of enemies, go greatly out of their way to avoid and to eliminate ill-will. They even have a spiritual tool to remove animosity, a type of incantation called a *digvghé:-hw(i)sdoʔdhí:yi* ("to make them to forget with").

139

It is obvious that spells of this nature have a wide use-fulness: in placating the anger of enemies and inadver-tently offended friends, in quieting family dissensions and lovers' quarrels, in influencing the outcome of law-suits, and in arranging satisfactory settlements of debts. In short, they can be of service in any situation wherein it is convenient to the user for someone to have a lapse of memory.

The *digvghé:hw(i)sdoʔdhí:yi idi:gawé:sdi* are for the most part used in "remaking" tobacco to be smoked and blown toward the target individual, and the knowledge of them is usually confined to medicine men. Theoreti-cally the tobacco can be prepared at any time and place, but it is much more effective if "remade" facing east by a stream at dawn, and if it is powdered with *tso:lagayó:li*.

This striking "forgetting" incantation to "remade" tobacco is said the regulation four times:

Now! *Ha!* It was our Mother in front of You and me: a smooth tree leaf.

You and I have just come to cut the eyes and the souls of the people in the Seven Clan Districts.

A great wind has just thundered over our souls four times.

Thought has just descended in a column, face downward, and has just joined their souls that have just sunk into the sea.

We do not know what spirit is addressed, since it is not mentioned by name, and the allusions to "our Mother" and the "smooth tree leaf" are equally vague.

Tobacco "remade" with the *i:gawé:sdi* below not only

produces a memory failure, but also causes the victim to be afraid of the smoker, states a footnote to the spell in the big ledger in which it was found neatly written.

I am like Something: I am like a Person.

You have come from under the Great Thicket.

I am like that Large Snake; I am like that Fuzz; I am like that thoroughgoing Wizard.

You have come from under the Very Large Mountains.

I am like that thoroughgoing Wizard, the Little Person; I am like that Yellow Man from Above; I am like that thoroughgoing Wizard from Above.

Black Yellow Mockingbird, You have just come to disquiet them.

You disquiet them!

While some of this text bears uncommon allusions (the "Large Snake" and "Fuzz" may relate to some myth now lost), spirits are frequently conceived of as deriving from the "Great Thicket" and the "Very Large Mountains."

This next *digvghé:hw(i)sdoʔdhí:yi i:gawé:sdi* can be employed in two ways: to "remake" tobacco with, or else by simply saying it four times and then blowing the breath toward the prospective victims after each time it is said:

Now! Listen! This is your name ⎯⎯⎯⎯; this is your clan ⎯⎯⎯⎯.

He excelled in songs — but down below.

I excelled in songs — but up above.

The Seven Clans are not to climb over me.

My soul lives about in the Seven Heavens.

The Little Man, who is a great Wizard, and I are clasp-
ing hands.

The Seven Clans are not to climb over me: it is I!

The "he" referred to above who "excelled in songs [i.e.,
sung spells]" is, of course, the victim, whose name and
clan are supplied in the appropriate places. "My spells,"
infers the reciter, "came from Above; his did not: ergo,
I can overpower him."

Some *digvghé:hw(i)sdoꝑdhí:yi idi:gawé:sdi* are specifically for placating anger. One such of these, merely
said four times at daybreak for four days toward the
residence of the offended individual, concludes with the
echoism of a wild goose call:

The White Wild Geese have just come down to live.

Da:hl(v)! Da:hl(v)! Da:hl(v)! Da:hl(v)![1]

Other anger-removing incantations are said four times
while "remaking" tobacco. With this one, tobacco, the
smoke of which can be blown toward the irate individual
at any convenient time, is best prepared by the water at
dawn, but it is still effective if for some reason it must
be "remade" otherwise. *Tso:lagayv́:li* is an optional in-
gredient.

Black Hair!

Black Chair!

Quickly!

They are soft!

The exact meaning of this *i:gawé:sdi* is far from clear — a circumstance universally held to be of no moment whatever.

The same conditions for "remaking" tobacco hold for this example, one of extraordinary length:

1.

Now! You Red Man! Your resting place is in the Sunland.

You man, the One who eyes you has just passed by the settlement without striking a soul.

He has just come very quickly.

Let what He found be covered up!

2.

Now! You Blue Man! Your resting place is in the Cold-land.

You man, the One who eyes you has just passed by the settlement without striking a soul.

He has just come very quickly. You have just enveloped it in Blue Fumes.

Let what He found be covered up!

3.

Now! You Black Man! Your resting place is in the Night-land.

You man, the One who eyes you has just passed by the settlement without moving a soul.

He has just come very quickly. You have just enveloped
   it in Blue Fumes.

Let what He found be covered up!

4.

Now! You Brown Man! Your resting place is in the
   Southland.

You man, the One who eyes you has just passed by the
   settlement without moving a soul.

He has just come very quickly. You have just enveloped
   it in Blue — *Ha!* — Fumes.

Let what He found be covered up!

In this powerful word-painting the spirits from the
four directions that slip in to inspect the animosity do so
with such secrecy that they do not strike against, or
jostle, even so sensitive and perceptive an entity as the
human soul. "You have just enveloped it in Blue Fumes"
refers to the hate that is being nurtured.

Inducing Remembrance

If it be to the advantage of someone for a person to
forget, it follows that it might be to the advantage of
someone for that person to remember; therefore, there
exist spells to strengthen the recollection that has been
subjected to "forgetting" sorcery. These counter-spells
are usually called *tsige:gv:ghe:hw(i)sdí:ha go:hú:sdi*[2]
("when they are made by them to forget/something").

"Remembering" spells are exceedingly rare, and those
with which we are familiar are exclusively for "remaking"

tobacco in the conventional way to be used in the same fashion as for inducing a memory failure; however, one suspects that there exist, or that there once existed, incantations of this type to be merely said.

The opulence of the imagery of these "remembering" *idi:gawé:sdi* may be illustrated by:

Now! White Pathway, I am attired!

Black Yellow Mockingbird, You have just come to paint his heart.

Black Yellow Mockingbird, You have just come to leap upon his heart.

Red Thread, You have just come to wrap up his heart and to carry it all night; You have just come to untie the Thinker before he quietly goes away.

White Threads will be clinging to him like a web.

Now I assume that he is out of sight.

Black Evil will adhere to his legs, He says.

Another specimen is equally arresting:

The Black Men, those great Wizards who just arose in the Nightland, have just come to take away your soul. Seven!

They have just gone in through the Nightland, so that you will not know it.

They have just finished putting Seven Shadows over the Very Yellow Water.

They have just arrived, carrying your soul. Seven!

They are not to help you climb over. Seven!

The Black Men, those great Wizards, have just carried
away your soul. Seven!

The fact that the text has six divisions instead of the
standard seven need not be puzzling: unquestionably one
optionally opens or closes the incantation with the additional line "This is his [or your] name _____; this is
his [or your] clan _____." One notes that the interpolations of "Seven!" are written in, and that there are
four of them.

XV

Good Will

Good Will

Creating Good Will
In a Gathering

THERE IS a class of spells for compelling a gathering of people to be disposed kindly toward, and to accept, an individual who proposes to identify himself with the group. Not only does one of these create a general atmosphere of congeniality, but it specifically negates animosity in any individual already affiliated with the group, and counteracts any disposition that he may have toward making demands upon the one using the spell. In a sense, these spells constitute what might be called "anonymity" magic.

Some are quite mild, and without ceremony are merely said four times while going toward a convocation of people. This is representative:

Now! Brown Spider, You have just distributed my soul
   all about!

Black Spider, You have just distributed my soul all about!

Blue Spider, You have just distributed my soul all about!

Red Spider, You have just distributed my soul all about!

One suspects that the colors of the Spider-spirits represent an unconventional clockwise swing about the compass, which begins in the "brown" South, progresses
through the "black" West and "blue" North, and ends in
the "red" and triumphal East.

   Another specimen of the "merely to say" type is:

White Pathways are mine!

I am attired in White Pathways!

Black Yellow Mockingbird!

Yellow Mockingbird, You have just come to borrow
   his soul!

This is especially effective against an individual in the
group who may be nursing a grievance.

   This exceptionally beautiful example is for "remaking"
tobacco in the stereotyped manner to smoke amidst a
body of people that one desires to win over:

Now then! I am _____.

Ha! I have appeared to you Seven Clans standing there:
   I am not lonely.

I will be bantering with them; I will be laughing with
   them; I will be talking with them.

For the smoke of the Brown Tobacco has just come to

fill all your nostrils: you all are not to think anything of it.

Ha! Everywhere where all of you are looking, let there be a Blue Haze.

You Seven Clans, I have just come to gain something.

You all are not to think anything of it: the Brown Tobacco did it!

As one may well believe from the wording, this spell is adjudged to be uncommonly useful in a circumstance wherein the magician must travel from group to group and make friends in each gathering.

Should there be a critical necessity for swaying the sentiments of a group among which there are dedicated personal enemies, *tso:lagayv:li* and this text may have to be employed:

Now! White Yellow Mockingbird! *Ha!* Very quickly You have just come to "remake" for me the Red Tobacco!

You will be mingling with the Great Wind from the Four Directions: You are a great Wizard.

Ha! Now very quickly You have just caused him to fade away.

Now! Now Yellow Mockingbird, You are an overpoweringly great Wizard!

Ha! Very quickly You have just come to mix the Red Tobacco: You have just come to "remake" for me the Ancient Tobacco.

Now! The Seven Clan Districts are not to climb over us!

My clan is _____; my name is _____.

Removing Enmity

Ill will too deeply engrained to be dealt with by one of the *digʋghé:hw(i)sdoʔdhí:yi* incantations may require the use of tobacco "remade" with a far more authoritative variety of *i:gawé:sdi* that is usually referred to by some such designation as *an(a)dá:n(i)gwa:dhihí yʋ:wi yígi*. The translation of this phrase is a trifle difficult, for the literal meaning is "holders of anger, they /persons/ if it exists." Perhaps "holders of grudges" would be a satisfactory rendering.

Tobacco is "remade" quite conventionally with this type of *i:gawé:sdi,* and its smoke is blown toward or upon the personal enemy.

The text can be brief:

Brown Tobacco, now You Seven Wizards will be from the High Large Places.

People from the Seven Clan Districts who were Thinking Something, "All of your hearts!" I will be saying to all of you!

More commonly it is septempartite:

Now! Kingfisher!

You are a great Wizard.

Now You have just come to "remake" the White Tobacco.

You were a great Wizard.

You and I have just come to clutch it at the same time.

Now! We shall make our souls into one forever.

Now! You and I will be great Wizards.

It is obvious that the animosity is conceived of as being something like a *ts(i)sgo:ya* ("insect," or "worm") in the soul of its possessor. The Kingfisher is rather routinely called upon in Cherokee medicine to pluck out the spirits of *ts(i)sgo:ya* from the bodies of those suffering from what the white physician would diagnose as bacterial infection. The tobacco that produces amity and peace would quite as a matter of course be thought of as White.

Here is an additional specimen:

Now! Listen! You Purple *Ugh(a)dhe:n(a)!*

Ha! You are dazzlingly bright.

You and I are great Wizards.

Now! This I am named, _____, and my clan is

_____.

Now! No one is to climb over me: such is not to be.

Now! Red *Ugh(a)dhe:n(a)!*

In every Clan Seat all of you will be seeking me, all of you people of the Seven Clans who Think of me!

This *i:gawé:sdi* is short but strong, and *tso:lagayṻ:li* instead of ordinary tobacco is used with it:

Now Nearby here the Great Red *Ugh(a)dhe:n(a)* now wends His way.

Now! Now the glare of the Purple Lightning will dazzle the Red *Ugh(a)dhe:n(a)*.

Also this Ancient Tobacco will be as much of a thorough-going Wizard.

Now! The Seven Reversers looking at me will be dazzled by the Great Red *Ugh(a)dhe:n(a)!*

XVI

Suppressing Evil

Suppressing Evil  **XVI**

Preventing One's Doctoring
From Being "Turned Back"

SOMETIMES A *dida:hnvwi:sg(i)* becomes apprehensive that good work on behalf of a patient might be nullified ("turned back" would be the way the Cherokees express it) by some malicious person who might learn of it, through either natural or supernatural means, and the decision is made to cover up all spiritual tracks of the doctoring.

After the patient has been "taken to the water" at dawn, the *dida:hnvwi:sg(i)* sends him home. Then the *dida:hnvwi:sg(i)* says the prayer below four times, throws water over his head seven times, and sprinkles water all about the vicinity of where the "going to the water" ceremony took place. Then, as he sets out for home, he

157

walks abruptly against the succession of four trees that
are standing more or less in a straight line.

What he says is this:

Now! Listen! You rest Above, You Red Man!

I have just come to borrow Your attire.

All kinds of you will not slander me: Lightning will be
    barring me from them.

I am the image of Him alone: *Wa:hl(a)! Sayi:! Da:sd(a)!
    Sayi:!*[1]

Destroying "Night-Walkers"

The medicine man has far more effective weapons
against witches who are molesting his patient than incantations to keep them at bay; for he can trap and kill these
sv:no:yi ane:dó:hi ("night/walkers about, they") if he
chooses to do so. He "remakes" unadulterated *tso:laga-
yv́:li* in ceremonies performed at dawn, midday, and
dusk upon the same day, then early in the evening he
rings the patient's home with the smoke from this tobacco. Any witch in any guise who attempts to cross the
smoke-line dies.

Here is an example of one of these witch-killing *idi:-
gawé:sdi* :

Now! No one is to climb over me!

His soul itself over there will be broken as the Sun rises,
    this Thinker of me; in the very middle of the light of
    the setting Sun he will be broken, this Thinker of me!

I will have emerged from the Seven Clans.

Then I have just come to strike you with Small Arrows,
    with Small Arrows I have just come to strike you!

Then I have just come to strike you with Lightning!

Then I have just come to strike you with Thunder!

Then with Clay your soul will be broken!

"Remaking" Ashes
To Kill a Lycanthrope

In order to further his or her evil designs, a witch
sometimes assumes the form of an animal or a bird,
favorite guises being those of a wolf, a screech owl, or a
raven. One is entitled to suspect that any wild animal
that appears in the vicinity of a Cherokee cabin upon
several nights in succession, or any bird that flies overhead and calls at approximately the same time upon
several consecutive days, is a metamorphosed witch. If
there is a sick person in the household, suspicion assumes
a deeper hue.

Any person may know some protective measure against
a disguised witch, but, as we have said, a *dida:hnvwi:-
sg(i)* possesses weapons to destroy, not merely to repel,
one of these evil beings. One of his witch-killing techniques, especially useful to him in disposing of a human
being masquerading as a wolf, necessitates the use of
ashes from a fire of lightning-struck wood. He "remakes"
these ashes, and then bides his time until the lycanthrope
has appeared for three successive nights. If it appears
upon the fourth night, he puts the ashes in the palm of
his right hand and blows them toward the witch. Death
follows swiftly and inevitably.

The *i:gawé:sdi* that the *dida:hnvwi:sg(i)* uses, said four times, is this:

> Now! You Ancient White One!
>
> *Ha!* Very quickly I have just come to hear.
>
> In nothing do You fail.
>
> Now! Right now You will cut them in the middle of the throat!
>
> You Ancient White One! *(said three times)*

"Returning the Evil By Fire"

The "returning the evil by fire" is one of the *dida:-hnvwi:sg(i)*'s most terrible weapons against a sorcerer or witch. Its effect is instantaneous, irreversible, and unfailingly fatal. He will seldom, if ever, use it in the interests of a client who has been "shot" unless specifically requested to do so; if it is he himself who has been the victim, however, he will employ it at the earliest possible moment after his health, and therefore his power, has been restored.

Before leaving home to go to some secret place in the woods to perform a "returning the evil by fire" rite, he says, "I have regained peace!" At the spot which he has selected to perform what to him is a necessary and justified execution, there will be a large stone. This he moves in such a manner as to permit a fire of lightning-struck wood to be built under its overhang. Into this fire he puts the *ga:dhidv*, the foreign object that was "shot" by witchcraft into his body or into that of his client, and steps aside so that the smoke of the fire will not touch him. Then he says:

Now! *Ha!* He who Thought Something will himself take it back!

Ha! The giver of the injury will himself take it back!

As for me, this is my name, _____, my clan, _____.

Seven! I have regained peace!

The *dida:hnvwi:sg(i)* observes the movement of the smoke from the fire: if it hangs low to the ground, the home of the sorcerer is nearby; if the smoke goes high and bends, the enemy lives at some distance away.

Upon returning home, the *dida:hnvwi:sg(i)* says once more, "I have regained peace!" He then awaits receipt of the details of the forthcoming funeral.

XVII

Protection

Protection  **XVII**

Hiding

THE GENERAL PURPOSE OF *adí:sgahl(v)doʔdhí:yi* ("for one to hide with") spells is to make one invisible to any person or persons that one simply does not wish to encounter, for any reason whatever, but the specific application to any enemy is obvious. It is widely believed that some of the more renowned of the last-century out-laws, such as Zeke Proctor, Billy Pigeon, and Ned Chris-tie, were masters in the use of this type of *i:gawé:sdi*. Certainly all of these three were conjurers. The authors possess manuscripts in the autographs of these banditti to prove that they were.

Billy Pigeon (Wi:l(i) Tsuwo:yiga:li) was especially

elusive; in fact, he was never brought to justice.[1] Perhaps when cornered he pronounced four times the proper *i:gawé:sdi,* maybe the very one that is inscribed in a little notebook that once belonged to him:

> Now! You Man, there is Fire!
>
> *Ugh(a)dhe:n(a),* there is Fire!
>
> Purple Man, there is Fire!
>
> *Dhla:nuwa,* there is Fire!

Another *adí:sgahl(v)doʔdhí:yi* spell, written in carefully made bold Sequoyah symbols on a scrap of heavy wrapping paper, carries the curious direction to sit down before leaving upon a trip and "to blow [doubtless after each of four statements of the *i:gawé:sdi*] toward it [the destination?]":

Now! Listen! Black Mole, very quickly you have just come to hear.

Now! You and I are dressed as one: very quickly I have just come to burrow in the earth.

A "hiding" spell is sometimes called a *di:da:n(v)dí:-yisdoʔdhí:yi* ("to miss them with, one"), and that is the caption for an imaginative little incantation that came from the roadless wilds that overlook Tenkiller Lake from the west side:

Now! Listen! This is the way it is: the Wind will take me away, and no one but I alone will know it.

Trees! Trees! Trees! Trees!

It will be swaying them, and they will be with me.

Now I am a great Wizard: I am as much of a speaker as
   U:ya![2]

"He has just brought the *Ga:dhidv*[3] in front of my
body" in the ensuing example is unintelligible to a contemporary Cherokee. Perhaps it was equally so to the
long-dead conjurer who wrote it in a little hard-cover
red notebook. He had underlined the word *Ga:dhidv*
questioningly. One may be sure that he accepted it upon
faith, however, for he footnoted with something approaching relish: *"O:saʔni hiʔaʔ tsigo:hwé:la adí:sga-
hl(v)doʔdhí hiʔaʔ* [This which is written is excellent for
one to hide with]":

Listen, Little Deer,[4] I, _____, am as much a Wizard
   as You: I bypass the Seven Clans.

You Wizards out there, people will not recognize me.

I will pretend to be a leaf from a tree: people will see
   me, but they will carelessly step over me.

I, Little Deer, am as much a Wizard as You: I bypass
   the Seven Clans.

I am as much a Wizard as You Wizards out there beyond.

He has just brought the *Ga:dhidv* in front of my body.

The missile will go by upon the other side: people will
   not recognize my body.

Suppressing Slander

Even as there is magic to negate inimical thinking,
there is also magic to stamp out defamatory talking. It

has no special labeling; each *i:gawé:sdi* for this purpose is likely to carry some such vague caption as "someone will be unable to slander you," or "for someone to be unable to accuse you."

There is an interesting example of an antislander charm that begins and ends with some silly sounding syllables that are the Cherokee version of "Blah! Blah! Blah!" One merely says it four times and blows his breath after each saying of it toward gossipers.

"Wi:yani yani yani yani!"

Let it be broken!

All of you are thoroughgoing Wizards!

In the Second Heaven all of us at the same time will be walking about together.

"Wihayo:! Wahigwu!"

The imputation of wizardry to the defamers and the prophecy of attainment of the relatively low Second Heaven appear to be made in sarcasm.

In another example one is instructed to blow four times in the direction from which one has just come, and then to blow four times in the direction in which one is going. Apparently this text is said but once thereafter:

Red *Ugh(a)dhe:n(i)*, it ends!

Red Mountain Lion, it ends out there ahead!

You Seven Clans, all of you are not to Think Something about me!

Humbling an
Overbearing Person

Idi:gawé:sdi for the purpose of dealing with overbearing individuals are seldom seen in conjuring manuscripts. Their scarcity is explicable: they are but minor magic and readily available to the general public. A master sorcerer might know one or two of them, of course, but he is usually concerned with far weightier matters.

There is no ritual whatever necessary in one of these spells. One merely says, or thinks, it four times when a meeting with an arrogant individual appears to be imminent. The brash one suffers no damage, except to his self-esteem.

The *"De:ʔ! Luʔ! Luʔ!"* that concludes this sample appears to be a cutting onomatopoeia:

Now! Listen! From the White Mountains I arose.

I am not a person: I am a Yellow Person.

I come to cut off a strip from your souls.

De:ʔ! Luʔ! Luʔ!

And this one ends with two rumbles of thunder, two thunderclaps, and a lightning flash:

Listen! In the White Mountains I originated: I am a great Wizard.

On White Pathways my feet make their prints.

It will be raining upon the Pathway upon which someone will be coming.

They have just come to crumble his soul in the very middle of the Pathway.

Wa:hl(v)! Wa:hl(v)! Da:sd(v)! Da:sd(v)! Sami:!

Protection
Against "Thinkers"

The Cherokees conceive of most evil as being the result of human disharmony with Nature. Most of the interruption, or diversion, of the normal flow of natural forces they hypothesize as stemming from the nurturing by an individual of destructive emotions that exude an evil influence and achieve harmful results without the necessity of any implementing action.

The harboring of malign emotions is known in Cherokee religio-medicine by the circumlocutory term "thinking." The verb stem *-el-* actually has more of the force of "believing" than of "thinking": *ane:li:sgi* ("those who think"), therefore, are individuals who project evil toward other human beings by the power of thought.

Idi:gawé:sdi for the purpose of protecting oneself from *ane:li:sgi* are rather numerous, and they are likely to be strewn with passages of noble beauty. The knowledge of them is confined almost exclusively to the *dida:hnvwi:-sg(i)*, who use them to "remake" tobacco for clients who blow its smoke upon themselves.

This one is for "remaking" tobacco in the usual manner:

1.

Now! Listen! Yellow Man!

Ha! Very quickly they have just come to live with You.

Ha, then! They will be living with You everywhere.
Immediately devour all their evil souls! *Ya!*[5]

2.

Now! Listen! Blue Man!
Ha! Very quickly they have just come to live with You!
Ha, then! They will be living with You everywhere.
Immediately devour all their evil souls! *Ya!*

3.

Now! Listen! Black Man!
Ha! Very quickly they have just come to live with You!
Ha, then! They will be living with You everywhere.
Immediately devour all their evil souls! *Ya!*

4.

Now! Listen! Yellowish Man!
Ha! Very quickly they have just come to live with You!
Ha, then! They will be living with You everywhere.
Immediately devour all their evil souls! *Ya!*

It is rather obvious that the spirits are identified with the four directions in this sequence: East, North, West, and South.

The "Big Deer" (*Aʔhwe:gwa*) invoked in this *i:gawé:-sdi* is a spirit animal, not an animal spirit.[6] A footnote, prescribing the usual saying, blowing, and expectorating, tells us that the charm is "to free oneself from 'thinkers' ":

Now! Big Deer, You Great Wizard, now You and I are moving toward the scene of conflict.

Now, You Wizard, You have just come to "remake" me.

My body will be filled with You, Big Deer.

Your vestment will likewise be my vestment.

You are a great Wizard: I also shall be a great Wizard, forever.

This is my name, _____, my clan, _____.

Big Deer, now You and I have just come to "remake" the White Tobacco with Your Heart!

Another specimen, one of most felicitous wording, enjoins an out-of-the-ordinary ceremony; a note states: "This which is written is a powerful 'helper.' This is to help one against everything that persons think that is evil. This written is to 'remake' tobacco. Four times per day for four days it is to be 'remade.' From then on you put the smoke on yourself. That is all you do":

Now! You Brown Whippoorwill! *Ha!* Come over the Seven Clan Districts.

Then do not let them turn back now; let those Thinkers forget, those among the Seven Peoples who Thought Something.

Let them be covered with the smoke of the White Tobacco.

Now! Brown Tobacco, then I am a Brown Whippoorwill!

You Overcomer, You Wizard, now You and I will "remake" the Brown Tobacco.

Now! This is my name, _____, and my clan is _____.

Spread Your Wings over the very crown of my head forever!

Some countermeasures against "thinkers" require "going to the water,"[7] and in Cherokee thought, therefore, fall into the category of medicine, not under consideration here, rather than magic; however, this is representative of one of the prayers used:

Now! Listen! You Provider, shield me with Your Might!

You have just come to shield me.

Little Red People, You all have just come to shield me.

The Wizard People are not to let the Important Thing penetrate, and there will be peace in the Seven Clans!

Forcing an Undesirable Person
To Move Away

One of the hitherto unreported classes of *idi:gawé:sdi*, and one of considerable importance, is that usually recorded in manuscripts under the caption *diga:ghahʔ:-sdoʔdhí:yi* ("to remove them with, one"). The purpose of this type of incantation is to prepare tobacco for use upon someone, usually a neighbor or a member of the household, whose conduct is obnoxious. The tobacco engenders in him such a sense of loneliness and rejection that he moves on in search of a friendlier spiritual climate. He experiences no actual harm, and once he leaves, his depression vanishes.

Diga:ghahv́:sdoʔdhí:yi spells are adjudged to work as successfully upon a white man as upon an Indian, and perhaps more so. Since he knows no antidote, the white man is vulnerable to the full force of the sorcery. And since these *idi:gawé:sdi* seldom require the name and the clan of the victim, but only his mental image, a white man, who, of course, has neither name (that is, a Cherokee name) nor clan, is fair game. Against Negroes, who are notoriously difficult to conjure, one merely has to "work" a little harder than usual in order to achieve completely satisfactory results.

The tobacco in a *diga:ghahv́:sdoʔdhí:yi* spell can be "remade" by the person who plans to use it if he knows how to do it; if he does not, he gets a *dida:hnvwi:sg(i)* or a *dida:hnese:sg(i)* to prepare it for him. It is "remade" in the conventional way: at dawn, facing east at the water's edge, rolled and blown after each of four recitations of the *i:gawé:sdi;* but it is never held up to the rays of the rising sun. Sometimes, either for additional potency or because with the particular *i:gawé:sdi* used it is customary for this to be done, the tobacco is "remade" for four successive mornings.

This tobacco is smoked four times in one day, or four times per day for four days. There are no specified times for smoking it, although dawn, midmorning, midafternoon, and dusk are considered to be especially favorable occasions. If the intended victim is a neighbor, the smoker, every time he smokes, advances about halfway toward the home of that person and blows the smoke toward the undesirable one's house; if the offender is a member of the smoker's own household, it is usually possible to blow the smoke directly upon him surreptitiously.

In rare instances, due to some special circumstances, the "remade" tobacco is not actually smoked, but instead is strewn across a road or pathway that the prospective victim is certain to travel. Contact with the tobacco achieves the same, or nearly the same, result as contact with its smoke.

Diga:ghahv́:sdoʔdí idi:gawé:sdi are characteristically short and rather simple. This example, from an Adair County conjuring book, is both shorter and simpler than most; one must, however, "work" with it for four mornings.

>White Squirrel! *(four times)*

>Rabbit! *(four times)*

>*Gu:le! Hu! Hu! Hu! Hu! (four times)*

The last line imitates a dove. The word for this bird in Cherokee is *gu:le-disgo:hnihi* ("acorns, it is a crier for"); the dove's call sounds to Cherokee ears like *gu:le* ("acorn(s)").

The next example also has a bird call in it, that of a crow:

The Black Crow has just come to sink His claws into you.

Ha! Very quickly He has just come to hem you in.

Gha:! Gha:! Gha:! Gha[prolonged]!

Now you will be lonely and sad from this time on!

Similar to the above is:

Now! The Black Yellow Mockingbird has just come to sink His claws into the middle of your soul.

Now the Black Crows have just come to frighten you away.

They have just come to hem you in.

You will go about lonely through the Seven Clan Districts.

The following *i:gawé:sdi*, for use against several individuals simultaneously, is exceptional in that it bears a hiatus in the text for supplying the target names; also, one omits the rolling of the tobacco if this spell is employed.

Loneliness has just come to your houses, _____, _____, etc.!

I stand completely out in the very middle of a bright ray. In the middle I take my stance toward the Sunland.

Now! Then you Seven Clans, any of you who own property in the Clan Districts, He has just come to push it into the water's brink, without there being a chance of retaining it!

I am called _____.

As to the identity of "He," we are afforded no clue.

Protecting a House

While it is to be doubted if in all the world there exists a people less property-proud than the Cherokees, nevertheless they are strangely sensitive to the danger of leaving a vacant house unprotected. Their dominant fear appears to be not that some marauder might steal or tamper with their possessions, usually few and seldom of any considerable intrinsic value, but that prowling evil powers might be tempted to enter and linger. Upon leaving home, even for a fairly extensive period, the householder seldom locks his door, but he gives no little thought as to how best to defend his property.

Some houseowners build traps, so to speak, to catch and eject intruders, human or spiritual. One such snare is made this way: The brain of a yellow mockingbird (*huhu*), a creature of vast magical powers, is inserted into a hole, a half-inch or so in diameter, cut in a small ovate house gourd from which the seeds have been extracted; the gourd is then buried in the ground in front of the front door. The spirit of that formidable bird-wizard, the yellow mockingbird, deals with those who enter for no good purpose.

Another individual may dig a hole about a foot deep at his front gate, build a fire of wood from a lightning-struck tree in the cavity, and then when the fire has burned down, fill the hole up. Lightning-struck wood, impregnated with the power of Thunder Himself, generates a force capable of overwhelming any housebreaker.

The commonest method of protecting a vacant house is to ring it with the smoke of "remade" tobacco. The procedure for preparing tobacco thus is widely known among the laity, but should the householder not know it, he engages a *dida:hnvwi:sg(i)* to "remake" for him protective tobacco which he uses as follows: At sundown he goes to the east side of his house, puts the tobacco in his pipe, and then lights it; smoking steadily, he then slowly encircles the house counterclockwise four times, enclosing about an acre of ground. As he arrives at each cardinal direction, he pauses briefly, faces that direction, and emits a puff of smoke toward it.[8] It is not necessary for him to say anything. It is generally conceded that a smoke-ring from "remade" tobacco remains potent for approximately six months. Malevolent spirits greatly fear it, and the stranger (no doubt in ratio to the innocuousness of his reasons for approaching the house) who comes in contact with it is tormented with that depression of spirits called *uhí:soʔdí*, a melancholia produced only by witchcraft.

This *i:gawé:sdi* for "remaking" smoke-ring tobacco is said four times at dusk, not at dawn, as one rolls it counterclockwise. The tobacco used is shredded twist, sprinkled with a minute pinch of powdered *tso:lagayó:li*.

U:ya! You have the Red Tobacco.

The Little Red Men have just come to spoil its smoke.

They come from the Seventh Heaven.

They bear very fierce hooves.

They will thoroughly spoil it.

Run toward the Nightland; decide not to turn back!

Run *Du:!*[9] Get out!

No one that we know has been able to go any further toward the identification of the being who is addressed than "an evil earth-spirit"; but the "Little Red Men" who come to trample and spoil the demon's tobacco (i.e., to negate the spirit's power) are, of course, the Two Sons of Thunder.

Tobacco is "remade" precisely as above while using the following *i:gawé:sdi.* The verbal picture of the intruder who stands quaking amidst yawning black coffins while huge and hideous snake spirits slither up to inspect the motives in his soul is an uncommonly powerful one:

The Diamondback Rattlesnake has just come to look at your soul!

The Velvettail Rattlesnake has just come to look at your soul!

The Ground Rattlesnake has just come to look at your soul!

The Copperhead has just come to look at your soul!

Ha! Then your soul has just come to rest where the Black Boxes were waiting!

One may optionally elect to provide a protective for one's home if it be left vacant; but there is little choice in the matter if a member of the family falls seriously ill: for the progress of any case of grave illness is apt to be the record of bitter warfare with witches who, in various clever guises, seek to approach and to destroy the patient. During the critical phases of an illness, the sufferer's home is ringed nightly with "remade" tobacco, and members of the family and friends "work" throughout the night at the bedside. The patient is especially vulnerable to evil powers at night, but he is equally so should he fall asleep in the daytime.

Tobacco to guard the home of a sick person is "remade"

conventionally, but sometimes a few shredded cedar leaves are added to it.

The *i:gawé:sdi* stated below is a *dida:hnvwi:sg(i)*'s spell to "remake" house-guarding tobacco, and is not available to the laity:

Now! Red Velvettail Rattlesnake, You rest in the Sunland!

You have just come into my breast, throwing Your head from side to side.

Somewhere amid the Seven Clans he will sit, among those over there who think something.

With my saliva itself I have just come to strike all of you!

Your souls did not come bumping noisily by.

Ya:! Your souls did not come bumping noisily by.

All of you have just come to do thusly!

"Bumping noisily by" seemingly alludes to the knocking upon walls and roofs to which roving witches are notoriously given.

Another professional *i:gawé:sdi* of the same type reads:

Now! You Ancient Red One, You have just come to hear. Red Tobacco, I have just come to live with You.

Ha! *U:ya* is the sayer: He has the Seven Clans lying down upon the Pathway.

Ho! *A:tsha!* *Ho!* You have just come to use it.

Ha! They have just come to calm him.

Very quickly we all have just come to smoke the Red Tobacco.

Without making a bumping noise they just came down.

You have just come to loosen the Black Chair from their
hands!
Very quickly We have just come to turn it over for them!

Admittedly there are some obscurities in the foregoing,
notably: "You have just come to use it [the spiritually
infused tobacco, the 'Red Tobacco'?]," and "They [the
benevolent spirits invoked?] have just come to calm him
[the anxious patient?]" The image of the forces of heal-
ings and righteousness wresting from the hand of evil the
Black Chair of Death prepared for the sick is a singularly
powerful one.

The importance of lares in the culture of the Oklahoma
Cherokees is implied in the discussion of the Little Deer
in *Friends of Thunder* (pp. 141-44). This revered midget
spirit animal can be induced to take up residence in one's
home by the use of an appropriate *i:gawé:sdi,* usually
referred to as an *aʔhwú:sdi godhlvhí:soʔdí:yi* ("deer/
small, it/to 'remake' it, one") such as:

1.

Now! Ha! Ancient One!
(His Food is Black.)

You and I have just come into His soul in order to draw
it out.

In the Place of Your Saliva and Mine we are to dine upon
His Saliva.

2.

Now! Red Deer!

(His Food is Black.)

You and I have just come into His Soul in order to draw
    it out.

In the Place of Your Saliva and Mine we are to dine upon
    His Saliva.

3.

Now! Black Deer!
(His Food is Black.)

You and I have just come into His soul in order to draw
    it out.

In the Place of Your Saliva and Mine we are to dine upon
    His Saliva.

4.

Now! The Gate!
(His Food is Black.)

You and I have just come into His soul in order to draw
    it out.

In the Place of Your Saliva and Mine we are to dine upon
    His Saliva.

5.

Now! He is indeed full!
(His Food is Black.)

You and I have just come into His soul in order to draw
    it out.

In the Place of Your Saliva and Mine we are to dine upon
    His Saliva.

6.

Now! He has just been fully fed!
(His Food is Black.)

You and I have just come into His soul in order to draw
    it out.

In the Place of Your Saliva and Mine we are to dine upon
    His Saliva.

7.

Now! Small One!
(His Food is Black.)

You and I have just come into His soul in order to draw
    it out.

In the Place of Your Saliva and Mine we are to dine upon
    His Saliva.

The wording of the above, an example of one of the
rarest and most esoteric of all magical *idi:gawé:sdi,* is
exceedingly archaic. The incantation is to be delivered
at some uncommonly rough and rocky spot. A paraphrase
of its first section might read like this:

Your attention, please, Supreme Being!

Little Deer has been enchanted.

You and I have just placed him in our power.

Our joint spiritual forces will keep him in subjection.

In exchange for the discharge of his duties as a guar-
dian of one's household, Little Deer expects to be fed.
Insofar as we know, he has no particular preference as to
what he eats, but he does especially like to have his food

set out for him in the kitchen before the family with
which he lives retires for the evening. If not regularly and
adequately fed he will indicate his displeasure at being
neglected by sleep-robbing noisiness at night.

Another lar seemingly has not come to the attention
of the non-Cherokeean world. It is called *Tsusgv́:dag(a)*,
a term that does not of necessity mean anything in Cherokee. It may derive from some other language. This being
is "remade" as follows: The "worker" takes a chair to a
cemetery, recites an *i:gawé:sdi* suitable to his purpose,
and smears the blood of some wild animal on the chair,
after which he takes the chair home with him and places
it for a period of seven days in his smokehouse. Presumably the *Tsusgv́:dag(a)* is attracted to animal blood; for
it must be fed the blood of some wild animal once a
month, probably at the new moon.

The *Tsusgv́:dag(a)* is extraordinarily sensitive to the
presence in the household where it has come to reside of a
"thinker," and should this person stay overnight he is sure
to rest but fitfully as the result of the terrifying activity of
the tutelary spirit. A household that enjoys the services
of a *Tsusgv́:dag(a)* has no need of locking its door when
it goes upon a visit: the *Tsusgv́:dag(a)* is distinctly unfriendly to strangers without proper credentials. If the
household moves away, the lar will not go with it, but
will remain at its old home, to the discomfort of any other
family that might attempt to occupy the house in which
the spirit lives.

Notes

Notes

CHAPTER I

1. All Cherokee terms are written in the orthographic system known as Lounsbury-Kilpatrick, devised by Prof. Floyd G. Lounsbury of Yale University and the senior author of this book.

2. There is frequently some difficulty in deciding how to spell a Cherokee word disassociated from a context. In some circumstances the final vowel would be voiced and the high pitch would fall upon the last syllable.

3. When speaking English, the Cherokees employ the term "witch" for a *dida:hnese:sg(i)* of either sex.

4. Kilpatrick and Kilpatrick, *Walk in Your Soul,* pp. 4-5. "If I wished, I could use the same *i:gawé:sdi* for every purpose that there is," a medicine man once confided to us. "It is the intention in the heart, and the knowledge, that really count."

5. "To say them, one," the plural of *i:gawé:sdi.*

6. Synonyms found in manuscripts are: *tso:la o:sd(v)* ("tobacco/good, it"), *tso:luné:gv* ("tobacco/white, it"), and *tso:lusdí:i* ("tobacco/small, it").

7. From Mooney and Olbrechts, *The Swimmer Manuscript, passim,* and from various North Carolina manuscripts that we have seen, we get the impression that *tso:lagayv́:li* has been much used in curing rites by the

Eastern Cherokees. In Oklahoma manuscripts contemporary with, or predating those from North Carolina, it is prescribed but rarely indeed.

8. Conversations with medicine men persuade us that these days are preferred for the sole reason that white men appear to hold them in reverence, and, therefore, they possess inherent and catholic magical implications.

9. Lightning-struck wood, impregnated with the power of Thunder, a being whose status is of the highest in the hierarchy of spirits, is widely used in both medicine and magic.

10. The literal meaning of this word is possibly closer to "repaired, it" than to "remade, it"; the Cherokees themselves, however, when employing the word in a ritualistic sense, invariably translate it as we so translate it. There is no real parallel with the Christian doctrine of transsubstantiation. The tobacco does not become thought itself: it is merely infused with the spiritual quality of thought.

11. Any of the several verbs that have the force of "to bewitch" are seldom used in shamanistic shoptalk. Forms of the euphemistic verb "to work" are substituted.

12. *Vide* Witthoft and Hadlock, "Cherokee-Iroquois Little People," *passim*, and Kilpatrick and Kilpatrick, *Friends of Thunder*, pp. 79-95.

13. Published in Kilpatrick and Kilpatrick, *Eastern Cherokee Folktales*, p. 403.

14. *Vide* "For 'Rebeautifying Oneself.' "

CHAPTER II

1. There is probably a connection between this custom and the magical hunting masks of the North Carolina Cherokees (cf. Speck and Broom, *Cherokee Dance and Drama*, pp. 85-86).

2. "Cherry Tree-Place." The residents of this community formerly predominately spoke, and to some extent still speak, a distinctive dialect of the Cherokee language

3. This exclamation has approximately the same significance in Cherokee as it does in English.

4. There are some North Carolina Cherokee hunting charms in Mooney, "Sacred Formulas of the Cherokees," pp. 369, 374, and in Speck and Broom, *op. cit.*, pp. 87-96. For additional data on Oklahoma hunting magic see Kilpatrick and Kilpatrick, "Muskogean Charm Songs among the Oklahoma Cherokees," *passim*.

5. Mooney, "Sacred Formulas of the Cherokees," pp. 374-75.

6. The concept of one's name having some part of the very essence of one's personality and being is very strong in Cherokee culture.

7. *Aristolochia serpentaria* ("Virginia snakeroot").

8. *Asclepias venticillata* ("whorled milkweed").

9. *Vide* "Games and Gaming." *Uyú:gwil(a)*, incidentally, is the proper form of this word, but it is seldom used.

CHAPTER III

1. There is a rather longish wind-charm, labeled as are most of the examples of its kind in Oklahoma, *uno:le aʔdhe:sdíyi* ("to frighten away the wind"), in Mooney, "Sacred Formulas of the Cherokees," pp. 387-88. For a specimen of a charm of this genre from Oklahoma, see Kilpatrick and Kilpatrick, "A Note on Cherokee Wind-Controlling Magic," p. 204.

2. Probably one of the many names of one of the Sons of Thunder (cf. Mooney and Olbrechts, *The Swimmer Manuscript*, pp. 23-24).

3. Onomatopoeia for a distant rumble of thunder.

4. The moon is sometimes referred to ritualistically as "Grandfather," and the sun as "Grandmother," but we cannot identify with certainty the term "Uncle."

5. This rare exclamation apparently has the force of "Aha!"

6. I.e., "thusly."

CHAPTER V

1. *Vide* Mooney, *Myths of the Cherokee*, pp. 297-300, 458-61; Kilpatrick and Kilpatrick, *Friends of Thunder*, pp. 43-56.

2. The reciter is addressing himself.

3. The Cherokees have never been able to make up their minds as to the correct spelling of the name of their draconic monster. We have bowed to individual preferences.

4. The roll of distant thunder.

5. In many *idi:gawé:sdi* the correct name and clan of the reciter and of the target individual, if there be one, are reckoned to be of primary importance. Precise identification by means of name and clan pinpoints the individual, and lays bare the essence of his personality upon which spiritual action may be taken. One more or less automatically assumes that any *i:gawé:sdi* that falls short of having the prescribed four or seven lines has left room for the improvisation of names and clans of those involved in the magic of the moment.

6. The Supreme Being.

7. One of the aboriginal tribal festivals, held at the time of the first new moon of autumn, had the same designation.

CHAPTER VI

1. This quail-like spirit bird figures prominently in Oklahoma Cherokee erotic magic (*vide* Kilpatrick and Kilpatrick, *Friends of Thunder*, pp. 94-95).

2. Haas raises the question whether or not *gahl(i)ghwo:gi*, the Cherokee word for seven, was derived from the Creek word for this numeral, the true Cherokee designation, now lost, being taboo because of its sanctity (Haas, *Comment on Floyd G. Lounsbury's "Iroquois-Cherokee Linguistic Relations,"* p. 22). We have no evidence to offer in explanation of why the numeral seven is accorded its status.

3. A mythic hawk (*vide* Mooney, *Myths of the Cherokee,* pp. 315-16, 466).

4. The spirit is not identified.

5. This phrase, often seen in love-magic, means: You will keep your "white" (joyfully approving) eyes on me.

6. We cannot identify this bird call.

7. The call of a crow.

8. The call of a dove.

9. The call of a yellow mockingbird (chat).

10. A nativistic secret society (*vide* Thomas, "The Redbird Smith Movement," *passim*).

11. On unsubstantial grounds this term has been identified as a synonym for the sun, and its etymology hypothesized as "very important woman" (Mooney and Olbrechts, *The Swimmer Manuscript,* p. 20). Oklahoma Cherokee medicine men make use of a species of document that has never been reported. It is called a *di:ghahnawadv:sdi* ("to follow with the eye, one [plural action]"), and is a sort of key which renders archaic terms into contemporary Cherokee. One of these *di:ghahnawadv́:sdi* in our possession equates the above term with "beautiful woman."

12. Apparently the reciter supplies here the name of a clan to which known or potential rivals belong.

13. The primary purpose of *digá:dhlidhadi:sdi* magic is to induce somnambulism.

14. Mooney and Olbrechts, *The Swimmer Manuscript,* p. 155.

15. Probably the aboriginal war club.

CHAPTER VII

1. The spirit addressed is almost certainly the Provider.

2. The Provider.

CHAPTER VIII

1. Mooney, "Sacred Formulas of the Cherokees," p. 374.

2. Mooney and Olbrechts, *The Swimmer Manuscript,* p. 101.

3. The same term, *ugi:sdo:di,* is applied to the symbolic piece of cloth (formerly buckskin) presented by a client to the *dida:hnvwi:sg(i)* in a curing procedure.

4. Interpolations are written into this *i:gawé:sdi.*

5. The spirit of flowing water.

6. Mooney, *Myths of the Cherokee,* pp. 426-27.

7. Probably the Provider.

8. One suspects a textual corruption here.

9. See note 3, *supra.*

CHAPTER IX

1. The statements in Gilbert, *The Eastern Cherokees,* pp. 268-69, 337-38,

are especially valuable. The "mouth" appears to refer to the cup upon the ball stick.

2. There is a myth that is instructive (*vide* Mooney, *Myths of the Cherokee,* pp. 311-15).

CHAPTER X

1. We hazard the conjecture that these syllables, on first inspection quite meaningless, might be ritualistic for *I:niyo? agi:hl(i)gé:ni* ("let us [you and I] shoot him in the neck"). The stem of the verb that means to "shoot" a foreign object into the human body by means of magic is *–yo:–*.

2. Could this represent the mumbling of the gagged witness?

3. There are numerous references in the literature to various members of the family of Thunder.

4. The fugitive that is being sought?

5. The reciter and his spirit-helper.

6. The fugitives.

7. Even in everyday speech this has the force of "I will still be alive."

8. The symbol of outlawry.

CHAPTER XI

1. I.e., "You determine the life span."

2. The sons of Thunder.

3. Plural of *dida:hnvwi:sg(i)*.

CHAPTER XII

1. Cf. Mooney, "Sacred Formulas of the Cherokees," pp. 391-95.

2. I.e., the victim has become like wood rather than human.

3. The bark of a dog.

CHAPTER XIII

1. Cf. "Oho!" in English.

2. The sons of Thunder.

3. Onomatopoeic of the rolling of thunder.

4. There are two fighting-charms translated in Kilpatrick, *The Siquanid' Dil'tidegi Collection,* pp. 5-6.

CHAPTER XIV

1. *Vide* Mooney and Olbrechts, *The Swimmer Manuscript,* pp. 28-29. This word has a true plural, but it is not often used.

2. The symbol of counter-magic.

CHAPTER XVI

1. A thunder-rumble; a lightning flash; a thunderclap; a lightning flash.

CHAPTER XVII

1. For an account of Billy Pigeon's skill in hiding, *vide* Shirley, *Law West of Fort Smith,* p. 56.

2. *Vide* "Protecting a House."

3. The missile "shot" into an enemy by witchcraft. The relevance is not apparent here.

4. *Vide* Kilpatrick and Kilpatrick, *Friends of Thunder,* pp. 141-44.

5. This exclamation, more frequently seen in curing conjurations than in magical *idi:gawé:sdi,* has something of the force of "It is done."

6. *Vide* Kilpatrick and Kilpatrick, *op. cit.,* pp. 141-43.

7. *Vide* Mooney, "The Cherokee River Cult," *passim.*

8. The ceremonial blowing of tobacco smoke toward the cardinal directions, in contradistinction to the important place it occupies in the cultures of many American Indian societies, is but a minor motif in Cherokee medicine and magic. Another instance of its employment is in the *E:lohi Ga:ghusdv:d(i),* the rite for the preservation of the Cherokee people (Kilpatrick and Kilpatrick, " 'The Foundation of Life': The Cherokee National Ritual," *passim*).

9. This exclamation equates with "Shoo!"

Bibliography

Bibliography

GILBERT, WILLIAM HARLEN, JR.
   1943. The Eastern Cherokees. Anthropological Papers No. 23, Bureau of American Ethnology, Bulletin 133, pp. 169-413. Washington, D.C.
HAAS, MARY R.
   1961. Comment on Floyd G. Lounsbury's "Iroquois-Cherokee Linguistic Relations." In Symposium on Cherokee and Iroquois Culture, William N. Fenton and John Gulick, eds. Bureau of American Ethnology, Bulletin 180, pp. 19-23. Washington, D. C.
KILPATRICK, JACK FREDERICK
   1962. The Siquanid' Dil'tidegi Collection. Bridwell

Library, Southern Methodist University, Dallas, Texas.

KILPATRICK, JACK F., and KILPATRICK, ANNA G.

1964.   Friends of Thunder: Folktales of the Oklahoma Cherokees. Southern Methodist University Press, Dallas, Texas.

1964.   " 'The Foundation of Life': The Cherokee National Ritual." American Anthropologist, vol. 66, no. 6, pt. 1, pp. 1386-91.

1965.   "A Note on Cherokee Wind-Controlling Magic." Southern Folklore Quarterly, vol. 29, no. 3, pp. 204-6.

1965.   Walk in Your Soul: Love Incantations of the Oklahoma Cherokees. Southern Methodist University Press, Dallas, Texas.

1966.   Eastern Cherokee Folktales: Reconstructed from the Field Notes of Frans M. Olbrechts. Anthropological Papers No. 80, Bureau of American Ethnology, Bulletin 196, pp. 379-417.

1967.   Muskogean Charm Songs among the Oklahoma Cherokees. Smithsonian Contributions to Anthropology, vol. 2, no. 3, pp. 29-40.

MOONEY, JAMES

1891.   "Sacred Formulas of the Cherokees." Seventh Annual Report, Bureau of American Ethnology, pp. 307-97. Washington, D. C.

1900.   Myths of the Cherokee. Nineteenth Annual Report, pt. 1, Bureau of American Ethnology, pp. 3-576. Washington, D. C.

1900.   "The Cherokee River Cult." Journal of American Folklore, vol. 13, pp. 1-10.

MOONEY, JAMES, and OLBRECHTS, FRANS M.

1932.   The Swimmer Manuscript. Bureau of American Ethnology, Bulletin 99. Washington, D. C.

SHIRLEY, GLENN
  1961. Law West of Fort Smith. Collier Books, New York.
SPECK, FRANK G., and BROOM, LEONARD
  1951. Cherokee Dance and Drama. University of California Press, Berkeley and Los Angeles, California.
THOMAS, ROBERT K.
  1961. "The Redbird Smith Movement." In Symposium on Cherokee and Iroquois Culture, William N. Fenton and John Gulick, eds. Bureau of American Ethnology, Bulletin 180, pp. 159-66. Washington, D. C.
WITTHOFT, JOHN, and HADLOCK, WENDELL S.
  1946. "Cherokee-Iroquois Little People." Journal of American Folklore, vol. 59, pp. 413-22.